A VISITOR'S GUIDE TO JANE AUSTEN'S ENGLAND

Sue Wilkes

PEN & SWORD
HISTORY

First published in Great Britain in 2014 by
PEN AND SWORD HISTORY
an imprint of
Pen and Sword Books Ltd
47 Church Street
Barnsley
South Yorkshire S70 2AS

Copyright © Sue Wilkes, 2014

ISBN 978 1 78159 264 9

Printed and bound in England
by CPI Group (UK) Ltd, Croydon, CR0 4YY

Typeset in Times New Roman by
CHIC GRAPHICS

Pen & Sword Books Ltd incorporates the imprints of Pen & Sword
Archaeology, Atlas, Aviation, Battleground, Discovery,
Family History, History, Maritime, Military, Naval, Politics, Railways,
Select, Social History, Transport, True Crime, and Claymore Press,
Frontline Books, Leo Cooper, Praetorian Press, Remember When,
Seaforth Publishing and Wharncliffe.

For a complete list of Pen and Sword titles please contact
Pen and Sword Books Limited
47 Church Street, Barnsley, South Yorkshire, S70 2AS, England
E-mail: enquiries@pen-and-sword.co.uk
Website: www.pen-and-sword.co.uk

Contents

To Nigel, Lizzie and Gareth

Acknowledgements

I would like to thank my editor Jen Newby for her boundless enthusiasm, encouragement and advice. Fellow authors Michelle Higgs and Jane Odiwe's help, advice and moral support have been invaluable, too. I am also grateful to Roy and Lesley Adkins for their help.

I would also like to thank archivists David Tilsley of Lancashire Archives, and Lisa Greenhalgh and Linda Clarke of Cheshire Archives and Local Studies. Records held by Lancashire Record Office and Cheshire Archives and Local Studies, to which copyright is reserved, are quoted by kind permission. Thanks are also owed to the Library of Congress's Head of Reference Section, Prints and Photographs Division, Barbara Natanson, for her help regarding illustrations.

I would also like to express my gratitude to Martin Brayne of the Parson Woodforde Society for his aid, and for granting permission to quote from the Woodforde Diary. Any errors in the text are, as ever, my own.

Jane Austen's novels, which I have loved and re-read many times since my childhood, were the major inspiration for this book, and I have my parents to thank for my first ever copy of *Pride and Prejudice*.

Every effort has been made to trace copyright holders for images used in this work. The publishers welcome information on any attributions which have been omitted.

Finally, I must once again thank my husband Nigel, and my children Elizabeth and Gareth, for their unflagging help and support.

Introduction

This book is a visitor's guide to Jane Austen's England for a gentleman or lady entering the world of the middle or upper classes. Through their eyes you will experience the lifestyles of the men and women in the society which Austen knew and wrote about in her novels.

Austen lived in a highly stratified society, and as you immerse yourself in her world, you'll soon become aware of its many inequalities. Most of England's land, property and riches are concentrated in the hands of a tiny minority; the social order seems ordained by heaven. His Majesty King George III is at the top of the social pyramid, followed by members of the Royal family. The portly Prince of Wales (1762–1830), 'the most finished gentleman of Europe', embodies the spirit of the age.

The Prince is notorious for his profligate lifestyle. He keeps mistresses, gambles away terrific sums and spends a fortune on his clothes and horses. The Prince became Regent in 1811 owing to his father George III's mental and physical illness (probably porphyria). The King is greatly loved by his people. It is common talk that his repeated bouts of illness have been exacerbated by the behaviour of his spendthrift sons. When his daughter, Princess Amelia, died in 1810, the King suffered a prolonged attack from which he has never really recovered.

Next in the pecking order are aristocrats and nobles, followed by the gentry, comprising baronets, knights of the shire, local squirearchy, and so on. Jane Austen and her family are middle class – a richly varied group including clergymen, farmers, professional men, and so on. The lower classes form the bottom stratum of society and many live in abject poverty and hunger.

Everyday life in England is overshadowed by years of conflict with France; the nation was also at war with America from 1775–1783 and again in 1812. The seemingly endless 'great war' is funded by taxation, which presses heavily on the labouring classes. Charity flows open-handed, however, from well-meaning members of the upper and middle classes like Emma Woodhouse in Austen's *Emma*, who considers it her duty to help those less fortunate.

Meanwhile the *haut ton* or *beau monde* enjoy a glittering lifestyle of feasts, balls, gambling and conspicuous consumption fuelled by the 'long credit' (sometimes of several years' duration) given by their tradespeople. The elite members of 'high society' have their own rules of style, dress and etiquette – not easy for an incomer to master, and woe betide the lady or gentleman who takes a false step.

But the defences of the polite world are not as strong as they seem. Money is the golden key which unlocks society's gates. The rise of industrialism has led to the emergence of affluent entrepreneurs and traders ready to spend their money on acquiring the trappings of gentility, such as the purchase of an estate, like Mr Bingley in Austen's *Pride and Prejudice*. Mr Bingley's £100,000 fortune was amassed by his father in trade. And of course, a 'single man in possession of a good fortune must be in want of a wife.' A good marriage can be a stepping stone to higher things; an imprudent marriage may end in poverty or disgrace.

This book will help you find your feet in Austen's England, whether you are a fond parent hoping to launch your sons and daughters into the best society, a young gentleman or lady looking for love, or a traveller keen to enjoy all the amusements that the towns and countryside have to offer. A lady's life is far more confined and constrained than that of a man, and if you belong to the fair sex, you'll need a relative or servant to accompany you on your travels.

Peer through the sparkling shop windows in London's Bond Street; gamble at an exclusive gentleman's club; feel the heat of a crowded ballroom as you try out the latest dance. Hold on tight as your vehicle's wheels clatter over the road, while the coachman cracks his whip and sounds his horn. You know you've reached your journey's end as your post-chaise hurtles through a narrow entrance at an alarming speed and deposits you in the hustle and bustle of an inn yard, surrounded by coaches, whinnying horses, chattering servants, and luggage and bandboxes piled high.

It's time to begin our journey into the world of Elizabeth Bennet, Mr Darcy – and their creator, Jane Austen.

CHAPTER 1

Travelling in Style

*'It was a sweet view – sweet to the eye and the mind. English
verdure, English culture, English comfort, seen under a sun bright,
without being oppressive.'*
(Jane Austen, *Emma*, 1815)

New arrivals like you are overwhelmed by the sheer beauty of the
English countryside. A chequerboard of cornfields and verdant
hedgerows gives the impression of an immense garden laid out on a
grand scale. Lush green hills and fields are punctuated by cattle
feeding peacefully. The landscape is dotted with villages and small
towns: some prosperous with neat, new redbrick houses, others old
and decaying, their ancient stones arranged higgledy-piggledy fashion.

German visitor Christian Goede (*The Stranger in England*, 1807)
was greatly impressed by the: 'Noblemen's seats, consisting of superb
mansions in different styles of architecture; and parks, abounding with
deer; plains, rivers, lakes, rich meadows, and well-grown woods',
which formed 'one grand enchanting picture.'

THE 'GREAT WEN'
All roads lead to London, the bustling centre of the nation's trade and
fashion. Unless you have your own carriage, you'll travel by
stagecoach or mail coach, post-chaise or hired horse, breaking your
journey where necessary at an inn.

One of the best views of London is from Shooter's Hill on the Dover
Road. You'll see the River Thames winding through rich green
meadows against a backdrop of gently rolling downs: a bristling forest

11

of ships' masts betrays the presence of England's naval might. Visitors coming from the opposite direction, that is from the west, enter the metropolis via the Great West Road at Hounslow. From Brentford you'll find that it's now almost one continuous street to London. Thomas Pennant commented mournfully in *The Journey from Chester to London* (1811): 'The multitudes of heavy carriages... give a melancholy idea of the overgrown size of our capital.'

The sheer number of travellers on the road is incredible. In his *Letters from England* (1807), Robert Southey said there were: 'Horsemen and footmen, carriages of every description and every shape, waggons and carts and covered carts, stagecoaches... coaches, chariots, chaises, gigs, buggies, curricles and phaetons; the sound of their wheels ploughing through the wet gravel was as continuous and incessant as the roar of waves on the sea beach.' (Southey's book, a clever travel memoir, purports to be written by Spaniard 'Don Manuel Alvarez Espriella', so that he can discuss English life as if through a foreigner's eyes).

As you approach London you'll notice the great dome of St Paul's towering over a mass of lesser buildings. During the winter months you'll often see the city wreathed in thick smoke; it wears a more cheerful aspect in spring and summer. After your coach passes the green glades and fields of Hyde Park, you'll whizz past Hyde Park Corner, through Piccadilly and into the noise and bustle of the capital. Although the smoke from innumerable coal fires gives London's red-brick buildings a greyish cast, newcomers are impressed by its wide streets, clean pavements, wonderful shops, crowds of well-dressed people, and the lawns and gardens which enliven the city squares.

Upon arrival, if the coach drops you off a long way from your destination, order a licensed hackney coach and ask the stagecoach driver to ensure that a trusty person transfers your luggage into the hack. Beware of the helpful stranger who offers to help you unload your trunks, as ten to one he is a thief on the lookout for easy prey. When boarding a hackney carriage, have plenty of coins ready so that the coachman does not have to find change. Note the coach's number in case you wish to complain to the coach-office, and check that you don't leave anything behind when quitting the vehicle, as lost property is seldom recovered.

Those on a tight budget can hire hackney carriages by the hour, or for the day. The gentry and aristocracy also hire hackney carriages for convenience, or if they do not wish to advertise their doings to all and sundry by using their private carriage. Charges are 1s 6d for the first hour, up to a maximum of 18s for 12 hours. Hackney carriages are not particularly clean inside. Louis Simond (a Frenchman who lived in America for over 20 years) was surprised to find straw spread over the floor of the first London hackney carriage into which he ventured. In his *Journal of a Tour* (1817) he noted that although the straw was changed daily it looked 'very shabby', but was better than 'a filthy carpet'.

So hackney carriages are rather looked down on. *Northanger Abbey*'s Catherine Morland can't sink much lower than this: 'A heroine in a hack post-chaise is such a blow upon sentiment, as no attempt at grandeur or pathos can withstand.'

Alternatively you can appear respectable by hiring a so-called 'glass coach' from a hackney-coach firm, as John Trusler recommends in his *London Adviser and Guide* (1790): 'A genteel coach, with glass windows, may be hired for the day... if bespoke, at the price of a hackney-coach; and if you have a greatcoat and hat for the servant to put on, it will be just the same as if he was your own servant.'

When going out, the immaculately dressed George Bryan 'Beau' Brummell (1778-1840) usually hitched a lift in a friend's carriage, or booked a glass coach. He only ordered a hackney carriage when in dire straits. One night, according to his biographer Captain Jesse, (*Life of George Brummell*, 1844), Brummell planned to attend a party at Lady Dungannon's, but his promised lift did not arrive, so he sent out his servant to order a hack. Brummell asked the driver to stop a little way from the lady's house and walked the remaining distance, happy that no one had noticed his inelegant transport. He was poised to enter the lady's 'splendid ball-room, already filled with guests', when a servant gently touched his arm, and said, "Beg pardon, Sir, perhaps you are not aware of it, but there is a straw in your shoe." The Beau was horrified.

CURRENCY

Please note that there are 12 pennies (d) to one shilling (s), and 20 shillings to one pound (£). (One shilling equals 5p in post-decimal currency). The gold coins currently in circulation are guineas (worth 21 shillings), half-guineas, and seven-shilling pieces. Gold sovereigns (worth 20 shillings) reappear in 1817, the year of Austen's death. Silver coins in use are crowns (five shillings), half-crowns (2s 6d), and shillings. 'Dollars' are Spanish coins countermarked (re-stamped) by the Bank of England in 1797 and 1804 to ease a shortage of silver.

Gold coins are often in short supply owing to the French wars, so in 1793 the Bank of England issued the first £5 notes; the first £1 and £2 notes appeared four years later. Banknotes are issued by provincial banks like that of Austen, Maunde and Tilson (Henry Austen's bank), as well as the Bank of England.

The silver three-shilling piece mentioned in Austen's *Persuasion* – the size of Mrs Croft's heel blister – first appeared in 1811. Silver groats (fourpence pieces), sixpences and pennies (from earlier in George III's reign) are legal tender but you are unlikely to find them in your change. When people find these coins they save them for their children because of their rarity value. In 1816 all silver coins in the realm were recalled to the Royal Mint and re-minted.

Pennies, two pence and threepenny bits, halfpennies and farthings (¼d) are copper coins. Each penny weighs an ounce (28.3g), so gentlemen's pockets feel very heavy when carrying a lot of change (ladies carry their money in a stocking-purse or a reticule).

HOTELS, INNS AND LODGINGS

You'll need somewhere to stay, unless your family owns a town house. If it's your first time in the metropolis, buy a good map or guide as it's all too easy to get lost in the endless maze of busy streets. The biggest and most elegant and expensive hotels in London are near St James's, Leicester Fields, and other places in the West End; fire and lighting (candles) are provided in these establishments. Hotel prices become more moderate further away from the West End. John Wallis's guidebook (*London*, 1814) warns that people planning to stay in

London for just a short time will find it 'expensive' but all classes of travellers are catered for, so that 'a skilful economist… may live at a tolerable easy rate.'

Some high-ranking gentlemen, including the Duke of Wellington, Lord Nelson and Lord Collingwood, prefer to stay and entertain at the top London hotels rather than gentlemen's clubs (see Chapter 5). The Clarendon Hotel is one of the most expensive: a dinner cooked by its French chef, Jacquiers, cost a whopping three or four pounds in 1814, plus a guinea for a bottle of claret or champagne.

If you can't afford a top hotel, you will find that the quality of inns varies considerably. Jervis and Kitchiner (*The Traveller's Oracle*, 1827) advised: 'The Elegance and Magnificence of some English Inns and Taverns, for instance, of the ALBION in Aldersgate Street, are equal to those of many Noblemen's Houses… but the generality of Taverns… are rather to be endured than enjoyed.'

When you have chosen a hotel or inn, the *Gentleman's Journal* for 1790 recommends that you try to secure 'a linen bed free from bugs, a chamber tolerably quiet, and a retreat to the street door or top of the house in case of fire.' Inn sheets are often damp. *The Traveller's Oracle* warned that the previous occupant of an inn bed may have been ill. The author recommended covering the mattress with 'a light Eider down Quilt, and two dressed Hart Skins' to act as a barrier against contagious disease. In Austen's *Emma*, the officious Mrs Elton's friend Selina 'always travels with her own sheets: an excellent precaution.'

It's a good idea to follow John Byng's practice. When Byng, Viscount Torrington (1743–1813) undertook several tours of Britain on horseback for pleasure during the 1780s, he sent his servant on ahead with the bulk of his luggage, including bed linen, to bespeak a good room for his master and arrange stabling for his horses.

When a gentleman enters an inn, he pulls off his boots and is given a pair of slippers to wear indoors. These 'slippers' are smelly, grubby old shoes with the heels removed, previously worn by dozens of earlier guests. If your hair needs cutting, the local barber will come to your room, or if a lady, a hairdresser or 'Frizeur' [sic] will dress your hair there, like the one who attended Nancy Woodforde at the Angel Inn,

London in June 1789. Her uncle, Parson James Woodforde, noted in his diary that his manservant Briton 'was well pleased with the Sight.'

A busy coaching inn is not a peaceful place to stay. A visitor to a Falmouth inn complained that it was never quiet: doors opened and slammed shut, bells rang (to summon service), people hallooed to the waiter from every room, and guests were constantly arriving or getting ready to depart. The whole inn shook whenever a carriage rattled up to the door. Robert Southey complained:

> The man who cleans the boots is running in one direction, the barber with his powder-bag in another; here goes the barber's boy with his hot water and razors; there comes the clean linen from the washerwoman; and the hall is full of porters and sailors bringing in luggage, or bearing it away; – now you hear a horn blow because the post is coming in, and in the middle of the night you are wakened by another because it is going out!

At busy times you may have to share a bed with a complete stranger if the inn is short of accommodation. On 7 August 1780, Parson James Woodforde visited Norwich, where he stayed at the King's Head, 'This being Assize Week the Kings [sic] Head was very full of Company – was obliged to sleep in a Room with a strange Gentleman an Attorney.'

You'll need plenty of ready cash to pay the inn servants. American Benjamin Silliman visited England in the early 1800s. In his *Journal of Travels* (1812) he noted that servants at:

> public-houses… are paid by the guests, and not by their employers [*the inn-keepers*]. They not only receive no wages, but many of them pay a premium for their places. The servants whom it is indispensable to pay in every public house are, the waiter, who has three pence a meal, the chambermaid, who has six pence for every night that you lodge in the house, and the shoe-black… called boots… receives two pence or three pence for every pair of shoes

16

and boots which he brushes. Besides these, the stranger who comes with horses pays six pence a night to the ostler, and the porter demands six pence for carrying in the baggage, and the same sum for bringing it out.

These sums are considered the bare minimum and you're expected to pay rather more than this. Any gentleman who attempts to leave the inn without tipping, whether by design or forgetfulness, will certainly be reminded by the servants not to forget them. It is also unwise to be too miserly when choosing accommodation. Silliman warned that, 'Londoners will not call on a man who resides in a dirty alley or dark court, for the impression is at once that he is not genteel.'

Generally, single gentlemen take furnished lodgings in private houses for half a guinea to three or four guineas per week, depending on the location. The poet and songwriter Thomas Moore (1779–1852), then a hard-up law student, stayed at George Street, Portman Square, in London during the spring of 1799. He paid six shillings per week for his accommodation, plus an extra two shillings per month for a servant to clean his shoes and brush his coat.

Apartments or lodgings normally comprise a bedchamber and parlour; some have an additional dressing room. Lodgers pay for their breakfast and tea but dine out. There are dozens of places to eat. A gentleman can buy a meal from as little as three pence at a 'slap-bang shop' or up to a guinea in a coffee house. Moore paid eight or nine pence for a meal out: he had 'soup, bouilli [*boiled beef*], rice pudding, and porter' for nine pence halfpenny, which he thought very cheap (Lord John Russell (ed.), *Memoirs... of Thomas Moore*, 1853).

Countrymen visiting London are in danger of being treated like 'country boobies' and overcharged by seemingly reputable shopkeepers and traders. The *Daily Journal* (1790) warned, 'This great town contains tens of thousands of excellent worthy characters' but also 'many thousands of miscreants who exist entirely by fraud or plunder.' You should 'keep your wits about you' when dealing with innkeepers, coachmen and tradesmen.

John Egerton (1796–1876), a Dorset clergyman's son, stayed in

London in 1826. He complained in his diary that he wanted to buy a particular type of carriage but was assured that 'such things were never seen' in London. He eventually found one to his taste at Morton's, a coach-maker in St Martin's Lane.

Some countrymen swiftly acclimatise themselves to the big city, as John Corry joked in his *Satirical View of London* (1815):

> They undergo a complete metamorphosis. The transition from the cool breezes that ventilate their rural retreat, to the warm atmosphere of the metropolis, affects those rustics with a malady that may be termed a brain-fever; under its influence they become delirious, and madly rush into the vortex of fashionable dissipation. The facility with which the squire adopts the modish dress, phraseology, effeminacy, and vices, of the town-bred rake, is almost incredible.

TURNPIKES AND TOLLS

From the capital you can board a coach to all the major towns and cities. Inns with mail coach services include the Angel Inn (St Clement's) and the Golden Cross at Charing Cross. Mail coaches to Bath, Exeter, Manchester and other places depart regularly from the Swan with Two Necks in Lad Lane. The speed and comfort of your journey across England will depend on the date and your route.

Road maintenance is the responsibility of individual parishes and turnpike trusts. Parish authorities provide labour and materials for a set number of days each year to mend local roads, but the increasingly heavy traffic means they cannot keep them in good order.

The first turnpikes were founded in the seventeenth century: a particular stretch of road was constructed by a private trust, and a tollgate set at each end to exact payment from those who used it. But people objected to paying to use the highway and so turnpikes were few and far between.

Many turnpike trusts were badly run; they skimped on materials or allowed their roads to deteriorate over time. In the winter even the turnpikes were shockingly dangerous; deep in mud, or full of vast ruts. Arthur Young, who travelled extensively in the late 1760s, complained bitterly about the roads in several counties. This is just one example from his journeys: 'The country from Tetford to Oxford is very disagreeable… The road called by a vile prostitution of language, a turnpike… is all of chalkstone, of which loose ones are everywhere rolling about to lame horses. It is full of holes, and the rutts [*sic*] very deep… The tolls are very dear, and considering the badness of the roads, vilely unreasonable.'

Long distance journeys were not undertaken lightly and some gentlemen made their wills before embarking on one. However, a concerted effort was made to improve the road system and two years before Jane Austen was born, new legislation made it easier for new turnpike roads to be constructed. By 1809 there were almost 23,000 miles of turnpikes.

Margaret Pedder, a Lancaster clergyman's daughter, recorded the tolls she paid in her travel diary when she travelled from Lancaster to London and back in the late 1780s. While travelling north after a night at Stratford-on-Avon, Margaret noted: 'Tuesday June 2… breckfasted [*sic*] set out five minutes before nine, Turnpike two and a half miles from Stratford £0 0s 9d got to Hockley House [*an inn near Birmingham*] & is a new house which divides the stage more equail [*sic*] stopd [*sic*] one hour and a half… Turnpike gate 5½ miles from Hockley House £0 0s 9d.'

In the early 1780s John Loudon McAdam's hard-wearing road surfaces made travelling more comfortable. In 1803 the Royal Chester coach left the White Lion in Chester at six o'clock in the morning and arrived in London at eight o'clock in the evening the following day. However, even the roads near London were still in a dreadful condition at that date.

The new 'metalled' roads constructed by John Metcalf ('Blind Jack' of Knaresborough) and Thomas Telford (engineer of the London-Holyhead road, finished in 1815) increased travel times and ensured smoother rides for passengers.

Away from the main roads, country lanes remain in as poor a

condition as the previous century. When Jane Austen's parents moved a couple of miles from Deane parsonage to Steventon Rectory in 1768, the lane was a 'mere cart track', so deeply rutted that light carriages could not travel along it. James Edward Austen-Leigh, in his *Memoir of Jane Austen*, records that Mrs Austen was poorly at the time (Jane was not yet born). To make the journey easier, Mrs Austen lay upon 'a feather-bed, placed upon some soft items of furniture in the waggon which held their household goods.'

Accidents are common when travelling. In a letter to her sister Cassandra from London (25 April 1811), Jane Austen describes a typical incident: 'Eliza [*Austen*] caught her cold on Sunday in our way to the D'Entraigues; the horses actually gibbed [*sic*] on this side of Hyde Park Gate: a load of fresh gravel made it a formidable hill to them, and they refused the collar... there was a sore shoulder to irritate. Eliza was frightened, & we got out, and were detained in the evening air several minutes.'

The risk of injury is very real. Parson James Woodforde (1740-1803) and his niece Nancy had a fright travelling from Frome to Bath in 1793: 'on a sudden turn up the Hill we met with a large tilted London Waggon with eight horses in it and very heavily laden, and it being very narrow where we met it, the Driver of the Chaise in backing the Horses to avoid being drove over overturned the Chaise, but...we received very little Injury. Nancy's Face was a little bruised...we were afraid that the Waggon would have crushed us.' The travellers walked back to their inn and waited until the coach was repaired.

There are some careful coachmen, however. From 1815 onwards, Charles Holmes was the driver and part-owner of the Blenheim coach which ran from Woodstock to London. Holmes drove the coach for 65 miles every day for two decades without a single accident. His grateful passengers clubbed together to present him with a magnificent cup of silver plate embellished with a coach and horses.

The number of passengers a coach is allowed to carry inside and out is painted on the outside, along with the owner's name. But passengers can still be overcrowded. When Parson Woodforde and Nancy set off for Bath from the Angel Inn, London in June 1793, their coach only held four passengers: 'We had a very fat Woman with a Dog and many bandboxes, which much incommoded us, and also a poor sickly good kind of a Man that went with us. We breakfasted at Maidenhead on coffee and tea.' Woodforde's servant Briton rode on top of the coach.

Conditions are just as cramped in large vehicles. Poet Robert Southey endured a journey from Worcester to Birmingham in 1807, in a coach designed to take 16 passengers:

> It is not very agreeable to enter one of these coaches when it is nearly full; the first comers take possession of the places nearest the door at one end, or the window at the other, and the middle seats are left for those who come in last... There were twelve passengers already seated when we got in... one woman exclaimed that she was almost stewed to death already; and another cried out to the coachman that she hoped he would not take in anybody else.

Southey compared the atmosphere inside to that of a prison: 'I never before passed five hours in travelling so unpleasantly.'

Stagecoaches halt several times along their route to take on and drop off passengers, causing annoying delays. Louis Simond travelled from Richmond to London in the early 1800s: 'We stopped more than twenty times on the road – the debates about the fares of way-passengers – the settling themselves – the getting up, and the getting down, and damsels shewing their legs in the operation, and tearing and mudding their petticoats – complaining and swearing – took an immense time.'

Night travelling is now more common than formerly. The poet John Keats travelled from London to Southampton in 1817. In a letter to his brothers dated 15 April, he recorded the things he saw from inside the stagecoach as its lamps illuminated the passers-by: 'Cow ruminating – ditto Donkey – Man and Woman going gingerly along – William seeing his Sisters over the Heath – John waiting with a lanthorn for his Mistress – Barber's Pole – Doctor's Shop… I popped my head out [*of the window*] just as it began to dawn.' (Sidney Colvin (ed.), *Letters of John Keats*, 1891).

An inside seat is more expensive than one 'outside' on stagecoaches, but preferable if the weather is inclement. Keats reassured his brothers: 'I am safe at Southampton – after having ridden three stages outside and the rest in for it began to be very cold.' Keats was lucky that he could change his seat. In February 1808 the *Edinburgh Annual Register* reported that two female 'outside' passengers on the Portsmouth coach froze to death when it lost its way in a snowstorm.

Many people love travelling despite the discomforts, but you'll endure some privations if travelling far off the beaten track. A writer in the *Monthly Magazine* (1 May 1820) advised his readers to ask their coach-builder to fit a 'substitute for a water-closet' when having a new closed-carriage built. In remote places like the Scottish Highlands, some of the smaller stages have no privy attached; even the inns in little towns often have no conveniences where you can relieve yourself, except a 'dirty exposed place'.

Genteel ladies rarely travel alone on stagecoaches unless they have no alternative. If Jane Austen wanted to make a long journey, she normally waited until her father or one of her brothers could take her. The author Mary Russell Mitford (1787–1855) was left in a very unpleasant situation in 1806 by her wastrel father. He abandoned her during a tour of north east England to help one of his friends go electioneering. She wrote to her father to: 'implore you to return… I call upon mamma's sense of propriety to send you here directly. Little did I suspect that my father – my dear, beloved father – would desert me in this manner, at this distance from home' (L'Estrange, *Life of Mary Russell Mitford*, 1870). Mary spent several anxious days before the runaway reappeared.

Mail coaches carry passengers and are the fastest way to travel. The Royal Mail service was overhauled in 1784, when entrepreneur John Palmer's plan was adopted of sending mail by coach, instead of post-boys on horseback. Mail coaches arrive in London at six o'clock each morning, and depart at eight o'clock each evening.

Coaches and coachmen are the heroes of the open road. Dashing young 'whips' dress as coachmen, and there is no greater treat for them than to sit next to the coachman on the box-seat and handle the 'ribbons' (reins). On special occasions such as May Day, or when there's important news like Nelson's victory at Trafalgar, the mail coaches and horses are festooned with ribbons and decorations.

When you travel by stagecoach or mail coach, the coachman and guard will expect a tip, usually a shilling each for 20 miles. Book in advance or you may not get a seat. When you join the coach, stow your parcels and luggage under the seat or in the boot unless you want them to get soaking wet and squashed.

The most luxurious way of travelling is by post-chaise, which you can hire from the innkeeper. You can reduce the cost by clubbing together with other passengers to pay the fare. Lucy Steele, in Austen's *Sense and Sensibility*, assured Mrs Jennings that she hadn't travelled to London in a common stagecoach: 'We came post all the way, and had a very smart beau to attend us. Dr Davies was coming to town, and so we thought we'd join him in a post-chaise; and he behaved very genteelly, and paid ten or twelve shillings more than we did.'

But travelling by post can be crowded too. Harriet Martineau recalled a journey from Norwich to her grandfather's house at Newcastle in about 1809 when she was seven years old: 'My mother... aunt Margaret, sister Elizabeth, Rachel, myself, and little James, aged four, and in nankeen frocks, were all crammed into a post-chaise, for a journey of three or four days.' (M. W. Chapman (ed.), *Harriet Martineau's Autobiography*, 1877).

If you prefer a smooth, quiet journey to the jolting of a stagecoach, you can go by canal boat instead: services run on several waterways such as the Chester Canal, Grand Junction, the Lancaster Canal and the Duke of Bridgewater's famous canal at Worsley, first opened in 1761. William Thomson recorded his jaunt in one of the Duke's boats in *A Tour in England and Scotland in 1785* (1788). The boat carried 'at least sixty passengers' and was 'perfectly commodious and convenient, having two cabbins [*sic*] in it, for the accommodation of different classes of people.' Any 'improper company' who misbehaved were set back ashore, with their money refunded.

ARRIVING BY SEA

England is a great maritime nation and many visitors come by sea. Travellers who need to make a long journey across Britain often sail around the coast instead of going by road. If arriving via the Thames estuary, it's best to leave your ship a few miles short of the capital and come ashore using a small boat. The waters of the River Thames are so crowded with ships that it can take several days for a ship to finish her passage. As you leave the vessel, the sailors usually give three hearty cheers to bid you farewell.

New visitors to these shores often complain of the rapacity of the customs officers, and you should have at least several shillings ready as a *douceur* (tip) if you wish your trunks and luggage searched and returned to you in a timely fashion.

When you disembark, you'll be surrounded by little boys quarrelling over the right to carry your luggage, and offering cards advertising the local inns. The inns have directories with the names and addresses of the chief inhabitants, so you can easily locate friends or business acquaintances. After you have landed you can breakfast at Dartford, for example, then hire a post-chaise to Greenwich, where you can break your journey at the Horse and Groom Inn, or change horses and carry on to the metropolis.

Alternatively you could try out the local food before travelling further. When Louis Simond landed at the port of Falmouth in 1809 he bought some hot rolls for breakfast and later had dinner in a hotel, where he enjoyed three small 'very good' but plain dishes, 'an English cook only boils and roasts.' Everything was clean: 'The table linen and glass, and servants' were 'remarkably neat, and in good order.'

However, Prussian visitor Charles Moritz complained about the 'scanty dinners' he endured on the road: 'Half-boiled or half-roasted meat, and a few cabbage leaves boiled in plain water, on which they pour a sauce made with flour and butter, the usual method of dressing vegetables in England.' (Moritz, *Travels Through Various Parts of*

England in 1782', British Tourists, or Travellers' Pocket Companion, 1814).

Moritz liked England's 'fine wheaten bread' with 'excellent butter and Cheshire cheese' although 'the slices of bread and butter, which they give you with your tea, are thin as poppy leaves. But there is another kind of bread and butter usually eaten with tea, which is toasted by the fire, and is incomparably good. This is called toast.'

Foreign visitors have some troublesome formalities to undergo at the customs house when they disembark because of England's war with France. You must show your passport to the customs officer, or give a written statement of your name, rank, former residence, and servants' names. The officer will issue you with a certificate of arrival. You must not leave the port without first getting a passport from the local magistrate or mayor.

Foreigners staying in London must take their passport and papers to the Alien Office at Crown Street, Westminster in London within a week of arrival (or if outside London, to the local magistrate). If you forget to do this you can be sent to prison.

PRIVATE CARRIAGES

Your place in the social pecking order is judged by whether you drive an elegant barouche, chariot, curricle, phaeton, or humble cart. A carriage is an expensive luxury for families on less than £500 a year. The Austens kept a carriage for a few years when the family lived at Steventon, but it was sold shortly before George retired. When Jane lived with her mother and sisters at Chawton, they kept a donkey carriage so they could visit the shops at nearby Alton.

Private carriages belonging to well-heeled or noble families have the family crest on the vehicle doors. In Austen's *Persuasion*, Mary Musgrove is very disappointed when she misses an introduction to Mr Elliot, the heir of Kellynch, because 'his greatcoat was hanging over the panel, and hid the [*coat of*] arms' on his curricle.

Aristocrats' vehicles are lavishly embellished. In 1792 the *Monthly Chronicle* reported that when the Prince of Wales attended the Queen's birthday celebrations on 18 January, his state carriage was decorated with painted emblems, including Britannia and Fame. The inside of the coach was lined with 'striped crimson velvet, adorned in the centre with an oval star, and his Highness's feathers [*fleur-de-lys*].' The coach's curtains were blue and fringed with gold lace.

Newly-weds may treat themselves to a new carriage to begin their married life. One of the biggest society weddings in March 1812 was the match between Mr Wellesley Pole and the fabulously wealthy heiress Miss Tilney (Tylney) Long. *La Belle Assemblée* (March 1812) reported that after the ceremony at St James's Church, Piccadilly, the happy couple drove off in, 'a new and magnificent equipage… it was a singularly elegant chariot painted a bright yellow, and highly emblazoned, drawn by four beautiful Arabian grey horses, attended by two postilions in brown jackets, with superbly embroidered badges in gold, emblematic of the united arms of the Wellesley and Tylney families.'

A barouche is very fashionable for town driving. It's a low slung, four-wheeled vehicle with two double seats facing each other, plus a box seat for the driver. In May 1813 Jane Austen had an enjoyable ride after visiting a picture exhibition in London: 'The Driving about, the Carriage being open, was very pleasant. I liked my solitary elegance very much, & was ready to laugh all the time... I could not but feel that I had naturally small right to be parading about London in a Barouche.'

Phaetons are private four-wheeled carriages driven by the owner. In Austen's *Pride and Prejudice*, Elizabeth Bennet's aunt, Mrs Gardiner, wishes for 'a low phaeton with a nice little pair of ponies,' so that she can explore the park at Pemberley in future. 'Highflyer' or perch phaetons have a very high seat over the front wheels, and large rear wheels. They are much favoured by the Prince of Wales, a noted 'whip'. If you visit Brighton you'll often see him driving his perch phaeton, sometimes drawn by four horses, sometimes six, along the streets or on his way to the races.

Dashing young men pride themselves on their skill with the reins. Racing curricles are very popular but their drivers often come to grief. In January 1812 William Cavendish (age 28), eldest son of Lord

George, had been on a shooting trip with his 18-year-old brother Charles near the family seat of Holker Hall, in Lancashire. Charles was driving William and his college tutor in a gig when the reins broke and the horse ran away. William was thrown out of the gig, landed on his head and died instantly.

The older generation, like Mrs Allen in *Northanger Abbey*, consider it improper for young unmarried ladies to travel alone with young men in open carriages. However, heroine Catherine Morland loved her ride in Mr Tilney's curricle: 'Henry drove so well – so quietly, – without making any disturbance, without parading to her, or swearing at them [*the horses*] – so different from the only gentleman-coachman whom it was in her power to compare him with! ... To be driven by him, next to being dancing with him, was certainly the greatest happiness in the world.'

Ladies can drive, although it's considered unladylike to control very dashing vehicles like high-perch phaetons. In *Mansfield Park*, Henry Crawford gives Julia Bertram a driving lesson in a barouche on their way to Sotherton, Mr Rushworth's seat. Captain Gronow (1794–1865) recalled that after the Peninsular War, many ladies were seen driving in Hyde Park 'in a carriage called a *vis-à-vis*, which held two persons. The hammer-cloth, rich in heraldic designs, the powdered footmen in smart liveries, and a coachman who assumed all the gaiety and appearance of a wigged archbishop, were indispensable.'

STAND AND DELIVER!
On your journeys you'll often see the rotting corpses and bones of executed malefactors dangling in the breeze. Criminals' bodies are hanged up in chains near the crime scene. Finchley Common, a notorious highwaymen's haunt near London, is frequently covered with gibbets.

This is the era of the so-called 'Bloody Code' of justice. By 1800 there were almost 200 capital offences on the statute books. A person can be hanged for stealing property worth 12 pence from a person, or property valued at five shillings from a house. In 1808 Sir Samuel Romilly succeeded in repealing the law which made stealing goods worth 12 pence a capital felony; the limit was raised to £15. Even children face capital punishment, although usually juries give them the benefit of the doubt. But children are hanged for serious offences like murder.

Despite these stringent penalties, highwaymen or 'knights of the road' flourished during the seventeenth and eighteenth centuries. England's most infamous highwaymen ended their careers on the 'fatal tree' at Tyburn long before Jane Austen was born, but their lurid exploits are still legendary. One of the most famous was Dick Turpin, 'long the terror of the North Road', hanged at York in 1739 for horse stealing (John Timbs, *Romance of London*, 1865). Turpin is now a popular hero: on 3 November 1819, Astley's Amphitheatre announced in *The Times* the forthcoming 'first appearance' of Mr Bradbury in 'an entirely new Equestrian Melo-drama [*sic*] founded on the exploits of the celebrated Richard Turpin, the highwayman.'

In addition to the threat of execution if caught, highwaymen risk being shot: mail-coachmen are armed with blunderbusses. Gentlemen travellers carry a gun with them when crossing areas infested by these mounted robbers.

Frederick Augustus, 5th Earl of Berkeley always carried a carriage-gun and brace of pistols when travelling after an incident in which a footpad fired a gun at him, which fortunately misfired. Berkeley was attacked again in November 1774: a highwayman stopped his post-chaise on Hounslow Heath. As the robber drew closer, his lordship calmly lowered the carriage window. The highwayman thrust a pistol inside, aiming at Berkeley's chest. But his lordship was ready and swiftly knocked the highwayman's pistol out of the way with one hand, firing at point-blank range with the other. The robber died instantly.

Highwaymen are no longer numerous but are still a force to be reckoned with. In 1793 there was one on the prowl not far from Jane Austen's Steventon home. A few years later the Rev Charles Powlett, who was well known to the Austens, fell victim to a Surrey highwayman and lost a valuable watch and money. People are far more afraid of footpads than highwaymen, however. Footpads are renowned for their viciousness because they cannot make a speedy getaway like horsemen; they may kill their victims so they cannot testify against them later. In 1793 Mrs Bramston, a friend of the Austens, was very distressed after being robbed and threatened by a footpad at gunpoint at Overton, not far from Steventon.

But you'll find that the age of the highwayman is drawing to a close. Coaches are faster and better protected, so robberies are decreasing. Travellers who need to carry large sums of money use bank notes instead of carrying tempting bags of gold.

To combat highwaymen near London, magistrates Henry and John Fielding introduced armed horse patrols, and a professional police force: the legendary Bow Street runners. Huge rewards were offered to anyone who helped arrest or convict a highwayman. Magistrates stopped licensing inns which harboured highwaymen. And as the heaths and commons where the lawless once waited for their prey were enclosed, highwaymen soon had no place left to hide.

Most coach passengers probably preferred to face a highwayman than the terror which struck the Exeter mail coach one autumn night in 1816. On 20 October, the coach had stopped at Winterslow Hut (an inn) to drop off the mailbags, when one of the leading horses was seized by a hungry lioness!

The lioness had escaped from a travelling caravan belonging to a menagerie. The passengers bolted into the inn for dear life while the coachman and guard tried to hold on to their kicking, screaming horses. Then a large mastiff appeared (possibly belonging to the lioness's keeper) and the lioness turned her attention from the horse, now bleeding and whinnying piteously, to the barking dog. A terrific fight ensued.

Luckily the menagerie keepers appeared on the scene and recaptured the lioness. 'Pomegranate', the poor horse who was mauled, was a former racing star and a valuable steed. The plucky dog and horse both survived their injuries. After a replacement horse was found, the Exeter coach was on its way again, less than an hour after this dreadful attack. Not even a hungry lioness could stop the Royal Mail for long.

29

CHAPTER 2

Gracious Living

'At that moment she felt that to be mistress of Pemberley
might be something!'
(Jane Austen, *Pride and Prejudice*, 1813)

The London 'season' is the busiest time of the year for socialites, and the nobility and great county families like Mr Darcy's in *Pride and Prejudice* keep a house in town. The 'season' begins early in the New Year and continues until early summer, when families decamp to their country retreats or fashionable watering holes like Margate. In autumn the 'little season' brings the upper classes scurrying back to London to enjoy a brief social whirlwind before winter fieldsports begin and they return to their estates.

However, in Austen's *Mansfield Park*, Lady Bertram's 'indolence' leads her to give up the town house 'which she had been used to occupy every spring', and remain in the country all year round, 'leaving Sir Thomas to attend his duty in Parliament.'

Most modern town houses in cities like London and Bath in the early 1800s have three or four storeys above ground level, with basements below street level containing cellars. According to *A View of London* (1804), generally the interiors of such houses are 'very commodious and elegant'. The windows are richly festooned with curtains; blinds prevent passers-by from looking in on the family.

In a typical town house the sitting room, breakfast parlour and dining room are on the ground floor. The best drawing-room, for receiving fine company, is on the first floor; it has the best carpet, and chandeliers hanging from the ceiling. The best bedroom is sometimes on this floor, too. The rooms above the first floor are bedrooms; servants sleep in the garrets at the top of the house, or maybe in the cellar. The kitchen is situated on the ground floor at the back of the house, sometimes in the cellar, and the stairs are at the back of the house.

If you don't own or rent a town house, then it's much cosier to stay with friends or family than at a noisy inn. When Jane Austen visited London she stayed several times with her brother Henry at Sloane Street, and at his later residence in Henrietta Street.

WATER AND 'GOING TO JERICHO'

Houses in the town and countryside are supplied with water from wells and rivers. In places like London and Macclesfield, spring or river water is piped directly into houses, or pumped into household cisterns. Robert Southey said that the water in London tasted 'abominable' and contained 'all the filth of the city'.

In London several companies, including the New River, London Bridge, Chelsea and Grand Junction (1811 onwards) provide the city's inhabitants with water. The supply is only turned on three or four times per week, and is often cut off at night. Also, some companies like the New River cannot guarantee sufficient pressure in the pipes (which are wooden) to supply customers with water above the ground floor or basement. According to a *Report...on the Supply of Water to the Metropolis* (1821), in 1810 the Chelsea Waterworks Company charged from 8s per annum for the lowest class of houses in its district to over 168s per annum for the largest properties. The company charged 12s annually for each water closet supplied, 6s to supply a single coach-house, and 2s 6d for each horse's stall in a livery stable.

In 1811 the Grand Junction Company began constructing new waterworks to supply the Paddington district. The new supply had sufficient pressure so that the inhabitants could enjoy the luxury of a water closet upstairs (in other districts people have water closets in the basement or on the ground floor, or out in the yard).

If your house has no mains water, and doesn't have its own well, your servants will fetch water from the nearest street or village pump, or buy it from a passing water seller's cart. It's rare for a house to have a fitted bathroom; your servant will bring you a hand basin of warm water for washing your hands and face. Water is carried upstairs by the servants from the ground floor or basement in pitchers, unless your house is equipped with a pump to force water up to a cistern on one of the upper storeys.

According to the *Annual Medical Review and Register for the Year 1809* (1810), a warm bath is thought 'effeminate... a "relaxing" and "enervating practice".' People like Beau Brummell and Count D'Orsay who take regular baths are considered rather eccentric. In his *Reminiscences and Recollections* (1862–1866), Captain Gronow recalled that his handsome friend D'Orsay 'took as much care of his beauty as a woman... He was in the habit of taking perfumed baths.'

However, as we shall see later, your medical practitioner may recommend a bath for your ailments. If a hot or cold bath is required, the servants will fill a hip bath with water for you, unless you purchase one of the new shower-baths (see Chapter 7). Your servants will have to empty your bath by hand, too.

During the winter the cold in rural districts can be so intense that all the water in the house freezes, including the contents of the chamber pots under the beds. On 28 December 1798, Parson Woodforde complained in his diary that it was so cold that: 'it froze in every part of the House – Milk & Cream tho' kept in the Kitchen all froze – Meat like blocks of Wood – It froze in [*the*] Kitchen even by the fire in a very few Minutes... Even the Meat in our Pantry all froze & also our Bread – I think the Cold was never more severe in my Life.'

Even houses in the middle of a large city are not exempt from severe frosts. When young clergyman John Egerton stayed in London, he wrote in his diary (10 January 1826): 'All the water freezes in my room at night – and some that was brought in the morning half an hour before I got up was caked over [*with ice*] before I used it.'

Your home may have a water closet installed, but this technology is not yet perfect. Water closets often give rise to unpleasant smells.

Very many houses are still equipped with an old-fashioned earth closet or dry-ash privy in the outside yard or garden, euphemistically termed the 'necessary-house', 'house of office' or, less politely, the 'jakes', 'bog house' or 'Jericho'. The snow was so deep in February 1799 that Parson Woodforde and his household were unable to 'go to Jericho.'

If your town house has an inside privy, or the cesspool is sited right underneath the house, sometimes its foetid contents begin fermenting and noxious gases can rise into your kitchen or parlour, unless a special pipe is installed in the cesspool vault to permit gas to escape. Not only is the smell offensive but the gases may oxidise (tarnish) the surface of your silver plate and metal fire irons.

When you rent or buy a town house, a trustworthy servant should check that the drains are clear, and that the cesspit has been emptied recently – otherwise your privy could overflow. Your manservant should locate the cesspool's whereabouts, but it's not always possible for older properties. *Trewman's Exeter Flying Post* (16 November 1820) reported a fatal accident at William Turner's house at Reigate, Surrey. A 12-year-old girl fell into an old cesspit which was under the scullery, unknown to the family; the flooring gave way, and the girl died.

There are no public conveniences in towns and cities, so when shopping you will either have to wait until you get home, or hope that one of the shops has a convenience for its customers – or you'll have to relieve yourself in the street. There are strict regulations about the emptying of necessary-houses and privies. This task, known as a 'wedding', is only permitted after midnight and before four o'clock in the morning, to avoid inconveniencing townsfolk with the nauseating smell. In the London area this task is expensive as well as disagreeable. In 1790 a typical price for night soil removal is five shillings per ton, and each cart holds about three tons. A servant should check the quantity of night soil taken away to ensure that you are not cheated.

If your house does not have a suitable back passageway so that the 'night soil men' or 'nightmen' can access the privy, they'll carry its repulsive contents through your house a bucketful at a time. Any 'nightmen' who carelessly drop any 'soil' in the streets are fined. The men expect to be treated to plenty of bread, cheese, beer and gin when they have finished their stomach-churning task. Cesspits are prone to leaking, especially if the surrounding rock is porous, so if your well is too close to your cesspool your drinking water may be laced with effluvia and your family will become ill from cholera and other nasty diseases.

There is no proprietary toilet paper on sale, so people use scrap paper or strips of newspaper. 'Bum-fodder' is a slang term for 'soft paper used in the necessary-house' (it's also a derogatory term for poor writing).

The privy is often sited at the bottom of the garden, so a lady will say that she is going to 'pluck a rose' when she needs to answer the call of nature. It's customary to keep a chamber pot under the bed so that one does not have to visit the privy in the cold and dark, or if the weather is inclement. These useful implements are also kept in the sideboard in dining rooms, ready for use by the men during dinner parties. Full chamber pots are removed and emptied by your housemaid or chambermaid. Invalids use a 'close-stool' or 'night-chair' for comfort during the night time. This is a wooden case with a hinged lid, which houses a chamber pot or removable porcelain bowl under a wooden or plush seat so that the invalid can relieve themselves whilst sitting at a comfortable height. Some close-stools are chair-shaped.

A physician, Mr Marson, argued in the *Medical and Physical Journal* (1803) that close-stools were smelly and unhygienic, despite being 'an elegant piece of furniture'. Even in the '[*sick*] chambers of the wealthy... the pan and contents only are removed... very frequently not until some hours after being used, during which time the wood is imbibing the putrid effluvia.' Because close-stools have a flat lid, they are used as an extra chair or table next to the sick bed. Marson suggested that close-stools should have a convex lid, so that people were not tempted to place barley water and other drinks on top of 'this nauseous putrid apparatus... directly under the nose of the patient.'

HEATING AND LIGHTING

During your stay you'll be warmed by a cheery fire in the hearth; fuel is wood or more rarely coal, depending on the district. Fire grates and fireplaces in gentlemen's houses are designed to show off their master's wealth: marble is an elegant choice, perhaps adorned with alabaster vases or flower stands.

Ladies should keep their muslin gowns well away from the flames when standing near the fire, as this material is highly flammable. The *Gentleman's Magazine* (January 1806) reported the tragic death of 13-year-old Mary-Ann, daughter of Thomas Grove of Ferne House, Wiltshire, after her muslin gown caught fire when she was alone in a room with her younger sister.

If clouds of smoke billow into your living room or parlour whenever the fire is lit, try installing a fire grate of Count Rumford's design; this miraculous invention is increasingly common. Austen's heroine Catherine Morland is disappointed when she first explores the General's home in *Northanger Abbey*: 'Yes, it was delightful to be really in an abbey! But… the furniture was in all the profusion and elegance of modern taste. The fireplace, where she had expected the ample width and ponderous carving of former times, was contracted to a Rumford.'

Candles are the principal form of lighting in the home; they are made from beeswax, tallow or spermaceti (whale wax), with a cotton or linen wick. Beeswax candles give the brightest, clearest light but are expensive. Tallow candles made from beef and mutton fat are cheaper, but give off a nasty odour and fill the room with acrid smoke.

In *Sense and Sensibility*, Lady Middleton asks Lucy Steele to 'ring the bell for some working [*wax*] candles,' so that Lucy can finish making a filigree basket for her ladyship's daughter Anna-Maria. When you attend a ball or other social event, your host or hostess will show off their wealth by using lots of candles.

In Austen's *Emma*, the impecunious Miss Bates is struck by how beautifully the rooms are illuminated when she attends Mr Weston's ball at the Crown Inn: 'This is brilliant indeed!... So well lighted up!'

she exclaims to her niece Jane Fairfax. 'Jane, Jane, look!... Oh, Mr Weston! You must really have had Aladdin's lamp!' In the same novel, social climber Mrs Elton dreams of giving a 'superior' card-party to outshine those already held in the village of Highbury, 'her card-tables should be set out with their separate candles and unbroken packs in the true style.'

Make sure that your family and servants don't waste candles; family members share them whenever possible. When Fanny Price, heroine of Austen's *Mansfield Park*, is banished to her old Portsmouth home, it's a mark of her father's boorishness that he hogs the only light available whilst reading a newspaper: 'The solitary candle was held between himself and the paper, without any reference to her possible convenience.'

The wick of a tallow candle must be constantly 'snuffed' (trimmed), so that the hot wax does not run ('gutter') down the side of the candle and be wasted. Snuffing reduces smoke, too. A tallow candle needs snuffing several times per hour. Candle-snuffers come in different designs: one of the commonest looks like a pair of scissors, with a box attached to one of the blades to collect the burnt wick as it is trimmed. Take care when snuffing a candle if you don't have a tinderbox handy. Catherine Morland gave herself a fright when she snuffed a candle too quickly on a dark and stormy night in *Northanger Abbey*: 'Alas! It was snuffed and extinguished in one! A lamp could not have expired with more awful effect.'

A tinderbox is commonly used to light a candle or fire in the hearth. This metal or wooden box contains a flint and piece of fire-steel, and the ashes of some burnt linen or a bit of rag for tinder. You strike the flint and steel together until they make a spark; let it fall onto the tinder to ignite it. Blow on the tinder until it smoulders, then push a match (a small piece of wood previously dipped in brimstone) into the tinder to light it. If the tinder is damp or the flint and steel of poor quality, it can be difficult to ignite.

In July 1810 a hapless maidservant at the house of Henry Spence, near Keswick, Cumbria suffered a terrible accident, according to *La Belle Assemblée*. The maid got up in the night to attend to another servant, who was ill. She could not strike a light because the tinder in her box was damp, but remembered being told that a little gunpowder would speed things up. She 'got the servant's powder horn, which he had to destroy magpies, and put a considerable quantity into the tinder box.' Her master's family were awoken by her 'dreadful screams' as her cap and handkerchief caught fire. They doused the flames and the servant survived.

Oil and gas lamps are used in well-to-do homes as well as candles. Following experiments with coal-gas for lighting in the 1790s, gas lights now illuminate streets, houses, factories and commercial properties. J. Appleton of 12 Ludgate St, London advertised his new gas lamps in Ackermann's *Repository* (1 October 1817): 'The much admired and improved One, Two and Three-light PATENT LAMPS, which are… so much in use for lighting Halls, Staircases, Dining-Rooms, Drawing-Rooms, Counting-Houses, Banking-Houses, Public-Offices, Churches, Chapels, Ball-Rooms, Public Places, etc. where a Brilliant Light is required.'

Your old oil lamps can be converted to burn coal-gas, but if you don't want to install gas apparatus, gas has forced down the price of lamp oil, as Appleton noted: 'J.A. having taken Advantage of the recent great fall in Lamp Oils, is enabled to supply his Friends and the Public with Genuine… Spermaceti Oil, for Patent and other Lamps, 4s 6d… Common Lamp ditto, 2s 8d per Gallon.'

NIGHTLY VISITORS
Bedbugs are almost unknown in country districts, but are pretty widespread in towns, especially in taverns. On 31 May 1782, Woodforde stayed at the Bell Savage Inn in London: 'I was bit terribly by the Buggs last night, but did not wake me.' The bedbugs did not deter Woodforde from staying there regularly when visiting London; on another occasion four years later he was so much 'pestered with buggs' at the same inn, he slept overnight in a chair with all his clothes on.

Even the most elegant residences are besieged by bedbugs. Whilst walking in the Strand, Benjamin Silliman was amused to see a shop sign announcing that its proprietor was: 'BUG DESTROYER TO HIS MAJESTY'. 'I had often seen the signs of his majesty's taylors [*sic*]; his majesty's shoemakers, etc... but this knight of the bedbugs had escaped me until now; no doubt this bug destroyer makes sure that the Royal slumbers shall not be disturbed by any of these rude vermin.'

So your housemaid should sweep under each bed daily; if not your place of repose will be home to a 'thousand nightly foes', according to Mrs William Parkes' *Domestic Duties: Or Instructions to Young Married Ladies* (1825).

At this date beds are of the traditional 'four poster' design, with heavy mahogany posts; or a 'tent bed' with an iron bedstead, with cloth curtains or hangings to keep out draughts when sleeping. Bed hangings are made of moreen (a mix of cotton and wool), or chintz lined with coloured calico. In *Northanger Abbey*, Catherine Morland is alarmed when the 'curtains of her bed' seem to move during a storm. The most soft and luxurious beds are made of feathers, but the linen covering (tick) should be very sturdy or the feathers will gradually escape and your bed will gradually shrink. A horsehair mattress is nice and elastic but not as warm as a woollen one. Each bed should have a bolster and two pillows; linen sheets and some Witney or Lancashire blankets will keep you warm and cosy.

COUNTRY HOUSES AND LANDSCAPES

On your tour of the countryside, if you apply in advance to the housekeeper you can wander round great houses and estates such as stately Blenheim House in Oxfordshire. You'll see a huge range of architectural styles, from the Palladian elegance of Chatsworth in Derbyshire, to the colossal Gothic tower of Fonthill Abbey in Wiltshire.

Within the last 30 years or so, William Gilpin's immensely popular works on 'picturesque beauty' have revolutionised the way we look at the landscape. As Gilpin explained in his *Observations on the Western Parts of England* (1808), 'picturesque beauty' means 'that kind of beauty which *would look well in a picture*. Neither grounds laid out by art, nor improved by agriculture, are of this kind.' Gilpin's works have launched a rage for exploring Britain's beauties during the summer months, as Robert Southey explained in his *Letters from England*: 'While one of the flocks of fashion migrates to the sea-coast, another flies off to the mountains of Wales, to the lakes... or to Scotland; some to mineralogize, some to botanize, some to take views of the country; all to study the picturesque, a new science for which a new language has been formed.'

The booksellers are awash with so many travel books steeped in the language of the 'picturesque' that a spoof has appeared: Combe's *Tour of Dr Syntax in Search of the Picturesque* (1809), illustrated by Rowlandson. Jane Austen seemingly enjoyed the hapless cleric's adventures, because she wrote to Cassandra (2 March 1814): 'I have seen nobody in London yet with such a long chin as Dr Syntax.'

Northanger Abbey's Henry Tilney is happy to give Catherine Morland 'a lecture' on the picturesque: 'He talked of fore-grounds, distances, and second distances; side-screens and perspectives; lights and shades;- and Catherine was so hopeful a scholar, that when they gained the top of Beechen Cliff, she voluntarily rejected the whole city of Bath, as unworthy to make part of a landscape.' Henry is 'delighted with her progress.'

Touring is also a good way for young ladies to learn about furnishings and absorb the tenets of good taste in preparation for when they have their own establishment. When *Pride and Prejudice's* Elizabeth Bennet wants to avoid meeting Mr Darcy at Pemberley during her tour of Derbyshire with her aunt and uncle, she claims that she: 'was tired of great houses; after going over so many, she really had no pleasure in fine carpets or satin curtains.'

But Elizabeth is delighted by Pemberley and its grounds: 'It was a large, handsome, stone building, standing well on rising ground, and backed by a ridge of high woody hills... She had never seen a place for which nature had done more, or where natural beauty had been so little counteracted by an awkward taste.'

Some of the last century's parks, with their stiff, formal layouts and long avenues of trees, look very old-fashioned now. When *Mansfield*

Park's bride-to-be Maria Bertram visits Sotherton, her future home, she declares that, 'there is some fine timber, but the situation of the house is dreadful... it is a pity, for it would not be an ill-looking place if it had a better approach.' An expert like Humphrey Repton can landscape your grounds and give them an up-to-date look.

You may be invited to stay at a friend's country seat. George Elers who later became a captain in the 12th Regiment of Foot, visited a 'modern-built mansion' in about 1815. (Monson and Leveson-Gower (eds.), *Memoirs of George Elers*, 1903). His friend John Vernon's Suffolk home, Wherstead Lodge, overlooked the river Orwell and had pretty gardens; Elers saw pheasants and hares playing in front of the windows. The Lodge was furnished in the latest style:

> The hall was light and elegant, and a flight of freestone steps on either side of it led up to the bedrooms, the double doors of which were faced with scarlet cloth, and the wainscots and wall were white picked out with a very light blue. There was a drawing-room... [*decorated*] with a beautiful Indian paper, pier-glasses to the ground. Florence vases and female figures were placed on the stands opposite the pier-glasses. They were of the purest alabaster, and were reflected back from the mirrors.

The house had two dining rooms; the most magnificent one 'was fitted up with a maroon paper, very rich, with silk curtains... and gold mouldings.' Both dining rooms were adorned with portraits of the Vernon family. Most unusually for this date, the Lodge had a 'commodious bath'.

Jane Austen's childhood home in the Hampshire countryside was more modest. Her father's rectory at Steventon had a front door which opened into a small parlour where Mrs Austen would sit busily making and mending clothes. A dining or common sitting room was at the front of the house, and George Austen had a study overlooking the garden.

Upstairs was another small sitting room or 'dressing-room' which, Jane's niece Anna Lefroy recalled:

Opened into a smaller chamber in which my two aunts slept. I remember the common-looking carpet with its chocolate ground, and painted press with shelves above for books, and Jane's piano, and an oval looking-glass that hung between the windows; but the charm of the room with its scanty furniture and cheaply painted walls must have been... the flow of native wit, with all the fun and nonsense of a large and clever family.

(W. & R.A. Austen-Leigh, *Jane Austen: Her Life and Letters*, 1913)

Over the years, the Austen ladies made several visits to Edward Austen (later Knight)'s elegant home at Godmersham Park. (Jane's older brother Edward was informally adopted by the Knight family in 1783; he formally changed his name to Knight in 1812). In a letter to Cassandra in 1808, when they were based at Southampton, Jane could not help contrasting Godmersham's comforts with their lodgings: 'In another week I shall be at home, and there, my being at Godmersham will seem like a dream... But in the meantime, for elegance and ease and luxury, the Hattons and the Milles' [*sic*] dine here today, and I shall eat ice and drink French wine, and be above vulgar economy.' (French wine is heavily taxed, and therefore expensive).

Jane Austen's final home from 1809 until her death was Chawton Cottage, a short walk from her brother Edward's occasional Hampshire residence, Chawton (Great) House. Chawton Cottage was a 'comfortable and ladylike' home with a 'good-sized entrance and two sitting-rooms', recalled Jane's nephew J.E. Austen-Leigh, although it was 'so close to the road that the front door opened upon it.' The cottage had seven first floor bedrooms and three attic rooms. It had a well by the bakehouse, while the Great House nearby had its own well and pump-house, from which water was pumped directly into the kitchen.

Rustic cottages embody people's sense of the 'picturesque' and fashionable gentlemen like to add charm to their country park with a cottage *orné*: 'No sort of building is more decorative to rural scenery,' a writer commented in Ackermann's *Repository* (1 August 1817). The Queen had one constructed at Kew, and the Prince Regent built Adelaide Cottage in Windsor Great Park, under the direction of the inimitable John Nash.

In Austen's *Sense and Sensibility*, the Dashwood sisters and their mother are forced to quit their home, Norland Park, after their father's death. They accept their relative Sir John Middleton's offer of Barton cottage, which has four bedrooms and two garrets, on his estate.

That conceited 'coxcomb' Robert Ferrars heartily approved of the Dashwoods' new residence, as he explained to Elinor: 'I am excessively fond of a cottage; there is always so much comfort, so much elegance about them.' But cottages are not necessarily charming to live in: when Willoughby begs Mrs Dashwood not to make any changes to their 'dear cottage', Elinor reminds him that it has 'dark narrow stairs, and a kitchen that smokes.'

EVERYDAY NECESSITIES
Meat is the staple diet of the upper and middle classes: beef, pork, lamb, and game, served boiled, or roasted to perfection on a turnspit before a blazing fire. As late as 1800, you will see dogs employed as turnspits in inns or country houses. The dog is placed inside a wooden wheel (like a treadmill) mounted on the wall. The wheel is attached to the meat-jack by a link or pulley; as the dog runs inside the wheel, the meat turns round and is evenly roasted. Large households keep two turnspit dogs, which work on alternate days.

Writer Edward Jesse (1780–1868) remembered seeing dog turnspits at work 'in the days of my youth' when being educated by a Welsh clergyman living in Worcestershire. 'They were long-bodied, crook-legged, and ugly dogs, with a suspicious, unhappy look about them, as if they were weary of the task they had to do, and expected every moment to be seized upon to perform it.' Alternatively, the spit is turned by hand, or by means of a clockwork jack, or a spring-driven 'bottle-jack'. Parson Woodforde employed several boy 'skip-jacks' over the years at Weston Longueville parsonage. They also did odd jobs such as drawing water from the well, helping with the harvest, and so on.

Your servants must keep your house and its contents scrupulously clean. It is under constant attack from vermin of all kinds. The meat for your household should be stored in a meat safe to keep out flies and mice. Even the most elegant kitchens have problems with vermin: a rat-killer was employed at Carlton House, the Prince of Wales's London residence, for an annual salary of £31 in 1814.

In January 1800 Woodforde was most discomposed: 'The Ham we had for Dinner today was almost devoured by the Hoppers getting into it, unknown to me before it came to table – The Maids and Nancy [*his niece*] knew it before, but said nothing at all to me about it.'

The dining tables of well-to-do rural families are supplied with fresh food from their farms and estates: grain, meat and vegetables for the table, fodder for the horses. Any surplus farm produce is sold to provide additional income. At Steventon Rectory, George Austen had a glebe farm (land attached to the benefice to provide an income), but it was quite small, so he rented nearby Cheesedown Farm to supplement the family's supplies. Mrs Austen kept an Alderney cow to provide milk and butter. In later life, when living at Southampton and Chawton, the Austen ladies grew fruit such as apricots and currants in their kitchen garden.

In *Emma*, Mr Knightley's estate manager, William Larkins, is very pleased when lots of apples are sold from Donwell Abbey farm. If you have plenty of land but little spare cash like Mr Knightley, you can dine on luxuries like fresh strawberries from the gardens. Rich landowners, like *Pride and Prejudice*'s Mr Darcy, have hothouses for growing tender fruits such as grapes, nectarines and peaches.

A caring landlord keeps rents affordable for his labouring tenants. Sir Robert Heron of Stubton, Lincolnshire, rented small plots of land to his workers at low rates so that they could grow vegetables and keep a cow.

In *Pride and Prejudice*, the housekeeper at Pemberley gives Elizabeth Bennet a glowing reference of her master Mr Darcy: 'He is the best landlord, and the best master... that ever lived.' Her praise makes Elizabeth warm to Darcy: 'She considered how many people's happiness were in his guardianship!' and 'thought of his regard with a deeper sentiment of gratitude than… before.'

In towns and cities, households are supplied by farms and market gardens; produce is brought in by waggon or canal boat, or on the hoof. In London hundreds of animals are driven to Smithfield market each day. Housekeeping can be cheaper in the city than the countryside. In a letter to Cassandra (5 May 1801), Jane commented on the cheapness of some provisions in Bath: 'meat is only 8d per pound, butter 12d, and cheese 9½d.' The price of salmon was 'exorbitant', however, at '2s 6d per pound the whole fish'.

Bread is very dear because there is a scarcity of grain; in 1800 the Royal household banned the use of flour for pastry in its kitchens. In a later letter (3 November 1813) Jane mentions: 'A fall in bread by-the-bye. I hope my mother's bill next week may show it.'

Highly perishable foods like milk are bought several times a day as needed. St James's Park in London is famous for its 'milk fair' held every fine morning from sunrise until 10 o'clock, as Sir Richard Phillips explained in his *Morning's Walk from London to Kew* (1817): 'A hundred mothers, nurses, and valetudinarians, accompanied by as many children' descend on the park to buy milk fresh from the cow. You may not want to linger, as the children scream loudly and the cows moo lustily to try and outdo them.

For some time now, household items such as candles, soap, salt, wine, ale, beer, malt, hops, starch, coffee and tea have been taxed to pay for the huge cost of the French wars. It's more economical to buy tea in chests rather than in small quantities. If you are the mistress of a household, keep expensive goods like tea, sugar, soap and candles in a locked storeroom so that your servants are not tempted to help themselves. In February 1790, diarist Benjamin Wyatt of Lime Grove, Caernarvonshire noted that he gave his wife 6s 9d to pay for tea.

The high price of tea, spirits and other luxuries has fostered a thriving black market in smuggled goods. Many otherwise law-abiding folk, even the upright Parson Woodforde and friends, see nothing wrong with contraband spirits. The local blacksmith 'Moonshine' Buck regularly supplied the parson with items such as smuggled rum, brandy and gin. On 12 October 1792 he confided to his diary that Buck was 'pretty easy fined' after a neighbour informed the authorities about a smuggled 'Tub of Gin' in the blacksmith's house. On 20 October, Woodforde noted discreetly that he paid Buck £1 13s 3d for 'divers little matters done for me' that year.

Country families like Parson Woodforde and the Austens brew their own beer and fruit wines. Brewing kills bacteria in water, so beer is safer to drink than water from a well or a river. Jane Austen and Cassandra made beverages like spruce beer at home, and Jane reminded her sister in a letter, 'The orange wine will want our care soon.'

An eighteenth century recipe for orange wine survives in Mrs Owen of Lancashire's receipt book:

> Take 6 gallons of fair water, put 12 pound of sugar an[d] the whites of 6 Eggs well beaten, bett em [*beat them*] 3 quarters of an hour then run it through a hair [*sieve*]... w'n [*when*] tis cold put to it 6 spoonfuls of zest... put in the juice of 20 Large Oranges but shave of[f] the Skins and yellow rind lett [*sic*] it worke [*sic*] 3 or 4 days.

The liquor was put into a large vessel and allowed to stand for a fortnight before being bottled.

SOCIALISING AND DINING

You'll begin your day writing letters, or perhaps going shopping before breakfast, which is served about half-past nine or ten o'clock. Ladies usually breakfast on a dish or cup of fragrant tea or coffee, chocolate and rolls or toast in the breakfast room, or in front of a roaring fire in the family library; or the servant may bring you breakfast in bed. Gentlemen tuck into heartier fare: eggs, fish and meat. Single men living in lodgings in London breakfast in a coffeehouse and read the papers.

The wealthier sort give 'public' (*à la fourchette*) breakfasts, which are grand social occasions. You'll dine on dishes of cold game, haunches of venison, salads, caramel baskets of bonbons, meringues, and delicious fruits and wines. These breakfasts are often given at weddings, with a bridal cake as the centrepiece.

After breakfast it's customary to go shopping (see Chapter 5) or make 'morning' visits until dinner, which can be late in the afternoon. If the family you are visiting are out (or are 'denied' by the servant), you should leave your visiting card so they will know you have called. In *Sense and Sensibility*, when Elinor and Marianne stay in town with Mrs Jennings, they know that Edward Ferrars has arrived in London because: 'Twice was his card found on the table, when they returned from their morning engagements.'

Morning visitors are received in the drawing-room and are offered refreshments. In *Pride and Prejudice*, when Elizabeth Bennet and her aunt pay a morning call to Miss Darcy at Pemberley, they are treated to 'cold meat, cake, and a variety of all the finest fruits in season'.

Dinner is a moveable feast, depending on whether you keep fashionable hours; country hours are normally earlier than in town. The *haut ton* do not dine until at least five or six o'clock, or even later. When Lady Newdigate stayed at Stansted Park in 1795, she commented that: 'The hours of ye family are what ye polite world w'd not conform to viz. Breakfast at 8½, dine at 3½, supper at 9 and go to bed at 10, but Everybody is at Liberty to order their own Breakfast, Dinner or Supper into their own Rooms and no questions ask'd.'

The Austen family dined at half-past three when living at Steventon Rectory in the 1790s, but over the years their dinner hour changed. While staying with the Bridges family at Goodnestone Farm in 1805, Jane mentions dining at four o'clock, so that they could go walking afterwards. Three years later, when the Austen ladies were living in Southampton, Jane noted in a letter, 'we never dine now till five.' During a visit to her brother Henry's new residence in Henrietta St, London, Jane wrote to Cassandra (15 September 1813) that soon after five o'clock, shortly after her arrival, the family sat down to 'a most comfortable dinner of soup, fish, bouilée, partridges, and an apple tart.'

Following dinner, tea and cakes are normally served around seven in the evening, and the day ends with a light supper and wine (unless one has dined fashionably late). As the dinner hour has got later and later, some people have a snack such as some cold meat in the early afternoon to fill the gap. By 1817 Sir Richard Phillips noted in his *Morning's Walk from London to Kew* that the dinner hour of the polite world had 'shifted to the unhealthy hours of eight or nine' at night.

ENTERTAINING

When planning a dinner or card party, set aside part of the day to organise menus, etc., with your housekeeper or cook. *Emma*'s new bride, Mrs Elton, complained: 'I believe I was half an hour this morning shut up with my housekeeper.'

If you are only serving one course, the company is told 'You see your dinner' when they sit down at the dining table. But for a special dinner party you should provide at least two courses. When *Pride and Prejudice*'s Mrs Bennet invites Mr Bingley and Mr Darcy to a family dinner at Longbourn, she: 'did not think anything less than two courses could be good enough for a man on whom she had such anxious designs, or satisfy the appetite and pride of one who had ten thousand a year.'

Mrs Bennet's dinner might have looked like this sample two-course dinner menu and table settings for August taken from John Perkins's *Every Woman Her Own House-keeper*, (London, 1796) (spellings as per the original). When a dish is replaced with another dish or course it is 'removed' (in this menu the soup is not a full course on its own).

DINNERS OF TWO COURSES

First Course
Soup santé, removed with

Tenderon of veal with parsley Fish sauce	Haddocks French beans	Rabbit collops
		Pickled mangoes
	Ducks and green peas	
Chicken pie		Mutton cutlets *à la Maintenon*
Pickles Lamb sweetbreads crumbed and fried	Sallad	Plain Butter Fricando of veal
	Roast beef	

Second Course

	Leveret roasted	Fricassee of mushrooms
Lemon pudding	Collared eel	
Grapes		Pine apples
	Salver with jellies	
Three pigeons roasted Plums		Fried smelts Cherries
	Potted lobster	
Apple fritters		Currant tart
	Two moor game roasted	

All the dishes for the first course are placed on the table at the same time. Then the serving dishes are 'removed' for the second course, which is laid in a similar fashion. Your guests eat a little of what they fancy from the dishes closest to them, perhaps asking a servant to pass them a favourite dish, if wanted, from the far end of the table.

49

More exotic meats are served at special feasts. Military man George Elers (1777–1842) attended a magnificent feast for 200 people in honour of the Marquess of Wellesley (brother of the future Duke of Wellington) at Willis's Rooms in 1806: 'All London was ransacked to procure all kinds of delicacies – turtle, venison, pines [*pineapples*], melons, peas – in short, everything in and out of season.' Elers paid 15 guineas for his meal.

Ladies who give a dinner party should be plainly dressed, so that guests do not feel inferior if only modestly attired; but for dinner parties you should always wear full evening dress.

When you give a ball, serve ices, lemonade, negus (spiced wine or port mixed with hot water) and rout cakes (small biscuit-like cakes, often flavoured with orange flower water, and sometimes iced) to your guests in between every couple of dances. It's usual to lay on a supper in a room adjoining the ballroom. In *Emma*, when Mrs Weston proposes just putting out a few sandwiches at the Crown ball, Emma and her friends think it 'a wretched suggestion. A private dance, without sitting down to supper, was pronounced an infamous fraud upon the rights of men and women.' For supper, delicacies like chicken, tongue, prawns and lobsters, trifles, ornamental confections and French wines are best.

You won't have to spend time slaving over a hot stove if you can afford the services of a good chef; in *Pride and Prejudice* Mr and Mrs Bennet 'were very well able to keep a good cook' and their daughters 'had nothing to do in the kitchen.'

You'll need a fine china dinner service from Derby, Staffordshire or Worcester for company, but a cheap plain set is best for everyday use, as china is easily chipped or broken by careless servants. In 1811 Jane Austen wrote to Cassandra: 'On Monday I had the pleasure of receiving, unpacking and approving our Wedgwood ware. It all came very safely.'

Your silver plate (perhaps a family heirloom) should be kept locked away when not in use as it is so valuable. Cut glass-ware is the most expensive for serving drinks but as it's thicker then cheap plain glassware it will be less likely to shatter and should last longer.

Your dining-room should be furnished with simple but sturdy mahogany chairs and tables; maroon or crimson curtains and carpets will give an air of opulence. Drawing-room and bedroom furniture is now far more comfortable than in former times; clumsy, unwieldy oak chairs and tables have been replaced by the light, elegantly curving designs by family firms such as the Chippendales and Thomas Sheraton. Furniture fashions change all the time: Grecian, Egyptian and Turkish modes have all been popular recently.

THE PRINCE'S PALACES

However you decorate your home, you're unlikely to match the lavish furnishings at Carlton House, the Prince Regent's London residence. According to Rudolph Ackermann's *Microcosm of London* (c.1808), the dining room alone at Carlton House is 'one of the most splendid apartments in Europe' with its red granite Ionic columns and walls covered with silver, and painted with Etruscan 'ornaments' in relief.

When the Prince took over the reins as Regent he celebrated with a splendid fete at Carlton House on Wednesday, 19 June 1811. The party was attended by over 2,000 people, including the Royal family and noble guests such as the Bourbons, the exiled French Royal family. The Prince was dressed in a field-marshal's uniform decorated with the riband and star of the Order of the Garter. (The King, to the Prince's chagrin, has never allowed him to go on active service because he is heir to the throne). The throne room of Carlton House was redecorated for the occasion with crimson velvet, gold lace and fringes. The state chair was placed under a canopy 'surmounted by golden helmets, with lofty plumes of ostrich feathers... the whole palace seemed a scene of enchantment.'

The main dining table which ran along the whole of the conservatory and across Carlton House, was 200 feet (almost 61m) long. Six inches above the table, as a centrepiece, a 'canal' flowed from a silver fountain. The canal 'banks' were adorned with artificial moss and aquatic flowers, and gold and silver-coloured fish swam through the bubbling water, which formed a cascade at the outlet.

Several bridges crossed the canal, one of which was surmounted by a tower.

Charles Abbot, Lord Colchester (the Speaker of the House of Commons) later commented: 'My children would have been amused with the river of water and the little gudgeons swimming about... and all the *grown* children were equally delighted.' The *Annual Register* (20 June 1811) reported that the dining tables groaned with 'every attainable delicacy and luxury, which wealth and rank could command, or ingenuity could suggest, and embellished by all the art and skill of the confectioner, with emblematical devices.'

The Prince, to do him justice, hoped to help British art and industry by giving this fête, which was ostensibly in honour of the poor mad King's birthday. The Regent's guests were asked to wear clothes by British workers: silk, lace etc. The Prince's table was covered with gold vases and salvers created by Royal goldsmiths Rundell & Bridge, and the table service was golden, too. Guests dined from silver-gilt plate. The unprecedented extravagance of this feast, at a time when weavers in Lancashire and Glasgow were starving, naturally gave rise to invidious comparisons.

Jane Austen was given a personal invitation to Carlton House in 1815. The Prince was a noted patron of the arts and literature and loved Austen's work. Jane was helping to nurse her brother Henry through a nasty illness when one of his doctors, who also attended the Prince Regent, realised that Jane was the author of *Pride and Prejudice*. One day he told Jane that the Prince 'often' read her novels and 'kept a set in every one of his residences.' Accordingly he had informed the Prince she was in London. His Royal Highness asked the librarian of Carlton House, James Stanier Clarke, to call on her.

Clarke duly appeared the next day and invited Jane to Carlton House, so that he could show her 'the library and other apartments, and pay her every possible attention.' Although Jane disapproved of the Prince Regent's immoral lifestyle, she felt unable to turn down this high honour. During her visit, Clarke declared that the Prince had given her permission to dedicate her next novel (*Emma*) to him, and upon publication Austen's publisher, John Murray, sent the Prince a handsome copy of *Emma* for his library.

The Prince has also squandered tens of thousands of pounds on his Brighton home, the Royal Pavilion. It is famous for its exotic domes and gorgeous interiors glowing with richly coloured Chinese lanterns, dragons, paintings and exquisite wallpapers.

At least one wealthy Englishman has tried to outdo the Prince. On 2 January 1814, the *Examiner* reported that Wellesley Long Pole was busy 'fitting up [*his home*] Wanstead House in a style of magnificence even exceeding Carlton House. The whole of the interior will present *one uniform blaze of burnished gold.*'

CHAPTER 3

The Latest Modes

'Woman is fine for her own satisfaction alone.'
(Jane Austen, *Northanger Abbey*, 1817)

It's essential to wear the latest styles if you don't want to look frumpy and *outrée* when out shopping or dancing. But the type of clothes you'll see being worn by fashionable ladies and gentlemen will depend on the date of your stay.

HIGH HEADDRESSES

If you visit in the 1770s you'll notice ladies wearing absurdly high headdresses. A triangular cushion or 'system' of horsehair three inches thick by nine inches diagonally, and seven inches in height, is fastened to the lady's head with 'black pins a quarter of a yard long', as Maria Edgeworth explains in her novel *Harrington* (1817).

On top of this cushion: 'the hair was erected, and crisped, and frizzed, and thickened with soft pomatum, and filled with powder, white, brown, or red, and made to look as like as possible to a fleece of powdered wool, which battened down on each side of the triangle to the face.' Next, 'curls', actually stiffened layers of hair 'rolled up into cylinders, resembling sausages' were placed on each side of the 'system'. Two or three 'curls' dangled 'from the ear down to the neck'. Then 'the hair behind, natural and false, plastered together to a preposterous bulk with... powder and pomatum, was turned up in a sort of great bag... or *chignon*.'

Finally, the mound of hair was crowned with a 'gauze platform with little red daisies, from the centre of which platform rose a plume of feathers full a yard high'; sometimes a jaunty 'fly-cap' or 'pouf' adorned with jewels or flowers was worn instead of the platform. Trend-setter Georgiana, Duchess of Devonshire took this uncomfortable fashion to extremes by wearing an ostrich feather 'one ell and three inches long' (122cm), a present from Lord Stormont.

The cost of hairdressing varies hugely. Parson Woodforde's niece Nancy was royally treated by their wealthy neighbours Squire Custance and his wife in 1782: 'Mr Custance sent after Nancy this morning to spend the Day with Mrs Custance and to have her hair dressed by one Brown, the best Ladies-Frisseur in Norwich... Nancy returned home about half past 9 o'clock this Even, with her head finely dressed... very becoming... Mrs Custance gave the Barber for dressing her Hair and Nancys [sic] the enormous sum of one guinea.' For comparison, the following year in Lancashire, Dolly Clayton of Lostock Hall paid 6d to have her hair dressed.

When wearing one of these weighty headdresses, remember to bend forward when going through a doorway or you'll lose your head! When travelling by carriage, sit on the floor or kneel down, otherwise you won't fit inside the vehicle.

You will be wearing your headdress for up to a month, so head lice may take up residence; a 'scratch-back' or back-scratcher comes in handy for relieving an itchy scalp. A scratch-back is a decorated stick carved from ivory, wood or horn, perhaps adorned with tortoiseshell. It's about a foot (30.5 cm) long and has a curved claw or 'hand' at one end.

WIGS AND WHIGS

A wig powdered with starch such as flour was *de rigueur* for gentlemen in the 1770s and 1780s; liveried servants and domestics wore wigs, too. Then the French Revolution came along. The writer Nathaniel William Wraxall pinpointed the 'Era of Jacobinism and of Equality in 1793 and 1794' as the death knell of formal dress for everyday wear. 'It was then that pantaloons, cropped hair, and shoe-strings, as well as the total abolition of [shoe] buckles and ruffles, together with the disuse of hair-powder, characterised the men.' Ladies cut off their long tresses, too, '"*a la Victime et a la Guillotine*", as if ready for the stroke of the axe.'

A scarcity of grain led to William Pitt's powder tax of 1795 (because flour was used for powder), and the wig's long reign ended. Clergymen below a certain income and the lower ranks of the army and navy were exempt from the tax. The Whigs were among the first to abandon their toupees to mark their opposition to Pitt's Tory party.

So if you visit England at the turn of the century, you'll find that both sexes wear their own hair 'cropped' (short) and un-powdered. A powdered wig is now old hat, unless you are a physician, a member of the armed forces or legal professions, or a clergyman like Jane Austen's father George.

The dramatist Frederick Reynolds (1764–1841) dated a change in manners to the wig's demise: 'Character and dress go hand-in-hand, and whilst the gay decorated head, marking the difference between lord and groom, lady and housemaid, gave a cheerful tone to society; [*sic*] the present republican cropt [*sic*] system not only levels all personal distinction of rank' but also casts 'a sort of Presbyterian gloom' over society.

'Natural' hair has its advantages. The *Spirit of the Public Journals for 1801* (1802) commented that the current 'more convenient and simple mode of wearing the hair... saves time and expense, does not soil one's clothes with grease or powder, and facilitates the perspiration of the head. This is the fashion *à la Romaine*, or *à la Titus* [*for men*].' However, a wig is warmer in winter.

Wigs have not yet disappeared altogether; in 1807 Robert Southey saw wigs of all styles and sizes displayed on busts with glass eyes in a London shop. The Hon Amelia Murray recalled that women not in the first flush of youth 'very generally wore wigs' even after the turn of the nineteenth century. 'The Princesses had their heads shaved, and wore wigs ready dressed and decorated for the evening, to save time... Widows almost always shaved their heads; my mother's beautiful hair had been cut off for her deep mourning, and she never wore anything but a wig in after years.'

Of course wigs are still useful for covering baldness; one of James

Beresford's *Miseries of Human Life* (1807) is 'finding yourself at least ten years *nearer to a wig*, than you had at all apprehended.' Try a liberal application of macassar oil or 'Russia Oil' (7s a bottle on London's Oxford Street) to relieve this embarrassing condition. Russia Oil allegedly stops hair turning grey, too.

Ladies wear short hairstyles, with a few curls or ringlets artlessly framing the face. Curling papers are used for styling. A maidservant usually helps with this task, as for Miss Woodhouse in *Emma*: 'The hair was curled, and the maid sent away, and Emma sat down to think and be miserable.'

Jane Austen clearly found hairdressing tiresome. In a letter to Cassandra (1 December 1798) she wrote: 'I have made myself two or three caps to wear of evenings since I came home, and they save me a world of torment as to hair-dressing, which at present gives me no trouble beyond washing and brushing, for my long hair is always plaited up out of sight, and my short hair curls well enough to want no papering.'

Young men like Jane Austen's brother Charles favour a short, cropped hairstyle, despite its republican connotations. Clergyman John Egerton paid 2s 6d for a haircut in London in February 1826, and invested 3s 6d in a pair of gloves, plus 1s for a toothbrush.

Men's curls are not always natural. Capt Gronow heard a good story (possibly apocryphal) about Lord Byron, 'a very handsome man, with remarkably fine eyes and hair', from one of his best friends. When Byron (1788–1824) was a Cambridge student, his chum, Scrope Davis, found the poet in bed one day with his hair in curling papers. Scrope cried: ' "Ha, ha! Byron, I have at last caught you acting the part of the Sleeping Beauty." Byron, in a rage, exclaimed: "No Scrope; the part of a d–d fool, you should have said… do not, my dear Scrope, let the cat out of the bag, for I am as vain of my curls as a girl of sixteen."'

DRESSED TO KILL

You'll have to change your dress several times daily. 'Undress' or *deshabillée* is worn at home. Slightly more formal, but practical, 'half-dress' or 'morning' dress is worn for morning visits and shopping.

When going to a formal occasion like a rout, assembly or ball, you'll wear your best gown – 'full dress'.

A visitor to England in the mid-1770s would see ladies wearing weighty silk and brocade sack gowns supported by great hoop petticoats and pads (false 'bums') underneath the skirt. They wear a large mob cap or a calash – a large hood stiffened with whalebone, which can be raised and lowered like a carriage-hood – over their huge headdresses when out walking.

In the early 1780s you'll notice ladies sporting enormous chip hats trimmed with ribbons and lace, and hoops are still worn. The *Lady's Magazine* reported in June 1781 that 'the full-dress gowns are made profusely long over large hoops. The petticoat trimmed richly with crape gauze... some silver fringe, and flowers with chains of ribbon. The sleeves are entirely of gauze, puckered, and buttoned up to the tucker.' Shoes had 'pearl buckles'.

Heavy silks and damasks were supplanted by more flowing styles and light, printed cottons for morning dress. Waistlines began to rise; ladies wrapped neckerchiefs over their neck and bosom, and young girls like Jane Austen and Cassandra wore wide sashes over their frocks. While Jane was growing up, hoop petticoats began to disappear, although they were still required wear for ladies at court throughout her lifetime. Jane's cousin Eliza de Feuillide wore a court dress with an enormous hoop when she attended a drawing room (reception) at St James's Palace in the spring of 1787.

Traditionally, English fashion followed Parisian modes. The French Revolution (1789) overturned fashion as well as society and ladies abandoned the courtly styles of the *ancien regime*. They adopted a simple 'Grecian' or 'classical' look with bare arms, and gowns as straight as a Roman column.

La Belle Assemblée (September 1807) recalled this startling change, led by the daring Mme Tallien of Paris:

> Nakedness, absolute nakedness, and nothing but nakedness, was therefore seen at the play-houses, at the opera, at the concerts, routs, and in public walks as well

as in private assemblies. When one lady left off a fichue [*a piece of linen pinned or tied across the bodice*], another laid aside a petticoat. When one uncovered her arms, another exposed her legs or thighs. Had the progress of stripping continued a little longer… French ladies would in some months have reduced themselves to be admired, envied, or blamed, as the Eves of the eighteenth century.

Mme Tallien's rival, Mme de Beauharnois, wore 'flesh coloured satin pantaloons, leaving off all petticoats' under a 'clear [*see-through*] muslin gown.'

If you stay during the 1790s, you'll see that although hoops have disappeared, English ladies still display petticoats under their gown, which is partly open. *Pride and Prejudice*'s Elizabeth Bennet has to 'let down' her gown to hide her petticoat after walking through the mud to see her sick sister Jane.

White muslin gowns are now a fashion staple: the elegant Miss Tilney in Austen's *Northanger Abbey* 'always wears white.' A fashion plate from the *Lady's Monthly Museum* (August 1798) shows a white 'round gown' for morning dress, with a long green net cloak and muslin bonnet. Dresses with trains are worn for morning and full dress. In the same novel, heroine Catherine Morland and her friend Isabella 'pinned up each other's trains for the dance,' but a few years later trains fell from favour even for full dress as gowns became shorter.

Muslin is delicate and you must be careful not to tear it. When Lydia Bennet elopes with Wickham in *Pride and Prejudice*, she asks her servant Sally 'to mend a great slit in my worked muslin gown.' A belle of circa 1800 wears a gown of clear muslin with a 'waistline' immediately below the breasts; the fabric is gathered under the bosom by a ribbon. Gowns button at the back. A white morning dress gown of cambric muslin, with a blue silk spencer, is suitable for promenading. Morning or 'walking' dresses usually, but not always, have long sleeves. At home 'undress' – a comfortable chintz or stuff gown and cap – is warm and practical when eating breakfast or writing letters.

By 1805 typical 'full dress', as featured in the *Lady's Monthly Museum* for June, is a gown of straw-coloured sarcenet (fine silk) with short sleeves, and a tunic of richly embroidered white crape. Short sleeves are *de rigueur* for full dress for another couple of years.

The fashion for short sleeves means that ladies afflicted with 'Superfluous Hairs' on the face and arms may buy products like 'Trent's Depilatory', advertised in *La Belle Assemblée* (December 1807) and sold by Mr Perrin of Covent Garden at 5s per box. It's 'highly approved in the first circles of fashion and rank' and 'removes the Hairs in a few minutes, and without injuring the Skin.'

The train's disappearance has had an unfortunate side effect, because diaphanous gowns are in fashion. Your bottom is practically on show to everyone, so if you are fundamentally modest, wear an 'invisible petticoat' to hide your nether regions. This is a band of very finely knitted material, tightly fitted so that it does not slip down, but which makes walking difficult. Luckily by the winter of 1807 trains trimmed with broad lace reappear for evening dress, although petticoats are now so short that gentlemen can see your ankles.

Gowns are very low cut. A waspish anonymous contributor to the *Monthly Magazine* (1 January 1808), newly returned to England after an absence of nearly 20 years, was appalled when he saw 'fashionable London belles' at the Opera House with their bosoms 'exposed in a manner I had never seen before, except under the piazzas of Covent Garden of an evening, or in some of the most nocturnal street-walkers.' He was even more shocked when dining with his grown-up nieces next day. They were 'all in the same state of *undress* I had observed at the opera, and even in more respects than I could have perceived there, as by means of modern *invisible petticoats* and transparent drapery, there were exposures below, as well as above.'

A belle of the *haut ton* can wear the most revealing fashions with little fear of censure. But middle class ladies in country villages must be more circumspect, unless you want to be the talk of your neighbours. In Maria Edgeworth's *Belinda*, the foolish Miss Moreton is persuaded by her friend 'to go to a public ball with her arms as bare as Juno's, and her feet as bare as Mme Tallien's' and to 'lay aside her half-boots, and to equip herself in men's whole boots; and thus she rode about the country, to the whole amazement of the world.'

Flimsy muslin gowns offer little protection against a British gale, so a pelisse – a long sleeved, full-length coat worn over a gown – will stop unsightly goosebumps. Parson Woodforde noted in his diary (18 November 1800) that the local squire's wife, 'Mrs Custance and eldest Daughter were dressed in brown Silk Pellices [*sic*], alias great-Coats – Emily Custance [*the daughter*] was dressed in white.'

Alternatively a mantle with a hood, or a cloak, a silk or muslin shawl, or spencer will keep you warm and snug. A spencer is a short (bodice-length) jacket with sleeves; in June 1808 Jane Austen found her kerseymere one 'quite the comfort of our evening walks.' Scarlet cloaks were fashionable for a time but in April 1809, *Ackermann's Repository* reported that this 'despotic dress' was now 'completely abandoned'.

Friends and family living far away from London are grateful for any fashion tips you can send them. Mary Russell Mitford wrote to her mother on 4 June 1809, 'Pale pink or pale blue pelisses are certainly worn, but mantles are far more stylish.'

NO KNICKERS!
Modest ladies wear a knee-length or full-length chemise with short sleeves next to the skin; daring society belles don't bother. You'll need to be proficient with a needle so you can sew your own chemises, unless you can afford a maid to make them.

Gentlewomen don't normally wear 'drawers' or 'pantaloons', as these garments are associated with masculine attire. Drawers end just below the knee. Ladies' pantaloons, which are almost ankle-length, first appeared at the turn of the nineteenth century. In 1804 the writer Augustus von Kotzebue mentioned a dashing young Parisienne who startled her fiancé by going swimming in a 'nankeen waistcoat and pantaloons closely fitting her body.'

Pantaloons are frowned on because they peek out from under a lady's petticoat, so are visible to the male gaze. In June 1806 some brave souls paraded in Kensington Gardens in cambric pantaloons with a train attached but no gown over them. Pantaloons briefly enjoyed some popularity, but quickly became unfashionable as they were associated with ladies of questionable morals.

Drawers are 'open' underneath (i.e. there are no full seams along the garment's bottom edge), which makes life easier for a lady when she needs to use a chamber pot. Manufacturers advertise drawers as practical wear for horse riding and for warmth. Ackermann's *Repository* for July 1817 contained an advertisement by Mrs Morris for her 'Ladies' Patent Invisible Dresses, Petticoats and Drawers' made from 'real Spanish Lamb's Wool, and India Cotton…a great preventive against colds.' But few respectable females wear them.

Stays or corsets are worn on top of your chemise. Your maidservant will lace you into your stays, which fasten at the back (stays for *embonpoint* ladies sometimes have lacing front and back). Stays are made from cotton or silk, with shoulder straps for comfort; the bodice is stiffened with whalebone or steel. You'll buy your stays from a staymaker, who will first take your measurements. In February 1781 Parson Woodforde's niece Nancy bought 'a new Pair of Stays' while on a 'Jaunt' to Norwich. Boys and girls wear stays, too: Mr Marston's Patent Stay and Corset Warehouse at Holywell Street in the Strand, London, as advertised in Ackermann's *Repository* (March 1818), sold adult and 'Children's Stays'.

Tight-lacing and stays were briefly abandoned in the late 1790s, when classical 'Grecian' styles were in vogue. There was a brief fashion for thigh-length 'long stays', which were also designed to push one's bosom heavenwards. In 1813 Jane Austen was very pleased to hear these stays were no longer worn as she thought it a 'very unbecoming, unnatural fashion'.

Corsets are here to stay, however, even though doctors like John Roberton (*A Treatise on Medical Police,* Edinburgh, 1809) warn against this 'barbarous' custom's reappearance. Tight-lacing is said to cause breast cancer, deformed ribs and spines, malformed digestive organs, 'shortness of breath', consumption, and 'frequent nausea and vomiting'. So if wearing tight-laced stays, keep a bottle of hartshorn (smelling salts) or lavender water ready in case you feel faint.

HATS, SHOES, AND ACCESSORIES

You'll need a bonnet or hat when out of doors. A young lady on a very limited allowance from her papa may not be able to indulge her passion for hats, however. The Hon. Amelia Murray remembered that a school friend, the daughter of the Chancellor, Lord Eldon, told her 'that she and her mother had one bonnet between them!'.

You can choose from a huge variety of bonnets; fashions are constantly changing, especially the width of the hat brim. A smart poke bonnet or straw hat, tied under the chin with a ribbon, is suitable for morning dress; in 1811 Jane Austen paid a guinea, which she thought inexpensive, for a 'straw hat, of the riding-hat shape'. Some ladies wear a mob cap underneath their bonnet. You'll see tall military-style silk hats, 'Minerva' helmets, and bonnets adorned with fruit or veils in the shops at various dates. In June 1806 ladies paraded in Hyde Park with 'hats and tiaras of white satin and various coloured silks', and 'turbans, bonnets and straw hats...tastefully ornamented' with roses, lilac and hyacinths, according to *La Belle Assemblée*. Over time, the brims on bonnets become wider and wider and by 1810 their wearers' faces were practically invisible.

Ladies often re-trim their old bonnets for a new look. *Pride and Prejudice*'s Lydia Bennet extravagantly buys a brand new 'ugly' bonnet which she thinks will be 'very tolerable' after she has bought some 'prettier-coloured satin to trim it with fresh.'

Caps are worn for 'undress' at home and for evening wear. While staying in London in 1813, Jane Austen asked milliner Miss Hare to make her a 'white satin and lace' cap, with 'a little white flower perking out of the left ear.' For 'full dress' you'll wrap a velvet or silk bandeau or filet, perhaps sparkling with diamonds, around your hair. A silk headdress or turban sporting a demure veil, jewels, or fluffy white ostrich feathers is very fashionable, too. When Catherine Morland attends her first ball in the Upper Rooms at Bath in *Northanger Abbey*, the ball-room is so crowded that she can see very little of the dancers except 'the high feathers of some of the ladies'.

You'll need long white kid gloves for attending balls and assemblies. It's traditional to begin the ball with a minuet, and your gloves should be spotless for this. Gloves don't need to be quite so immaculate for the country dances, but take two pairs with you just in case. Your shoes and gloves should match for day-wear; in 1807 lilac, straw-coloured, or lemon-coloured kid are fashionable. Short gloves are practical for horse riding.

Formerly ladies wore shoes with dainty high heels, but in the 1790s heels became much shorter and were gradually replaced with wedges. Heels virtually disappeared when satin pump-style shoes became popular for full dress at the turn of the nineteenth century. Now ladies' walking shoes or slippers are made from kid, velvet, silk or satin; laced Grecian sandals are worn at balls.

A pretty ivory fan is another must-have when going dancing: in January 1799 Jane Austen wore green shoes and carried a 'white fan' to Lady Dorchester's ball at Kempshott House, where she spent a 'very pleasant evening... there were more dancers than the room could conveniently hold, which is enough to constitute a good ball at any time.'

Your outfit won't be complete without some jewellery – perhaps a pearl necklace or some 'white beads' like those worn by *Northanger Abbey*'s Eleanor Tilney around her head. Jane Austen and Cassandra were thrilled when their brother Charles bought them 'gold chains and topaze [*sic*] crosses' with his prize money after his ship the *Endymion* captured a privateer. Jane wrote to her sister: 'He must be well scolded... We shall be unbearably fine.'

Stockings are made of silk for best, or cotton or wool for warmth; they are held on by a garter fastened round the knee. The finest stockings are embroidered, and decorated with 'clocks' (patterns). Jane Austen took great care to buy good quality silk stockings when shopping. A self-proclaimed fashion correspondent to the *Chester Chronicle* (14 September 1810) commented that the latest mode was: 'Pic-nick [*sic*] silk stockings with lace clocks; flesh-coloured are the most fashionable, as they have the appearance of bare legs – nudity being all the rage. The stockings carelessly bespattered with mud, to agree with the gown... should be bordered about three inches deep with the most fashionable coloured mud which can be found.'

When out walking, even in town, wear pattens to protect your shoes. The roads are covered with horse droppings and other nastiness. A patten is a kind of overshoe comprising a wooden sole with an iron ring underneath. This raises your foot an inch or two above the ground, and helps lift your petticoats away from the mud. Pattens are fastened over the shoes with ribbons or buckles. Pattens make an inelegant din: in his *Journal of A Tour* Louis Simond noticed how the ladies of 1810 moved 'with an elastic gait' on their pattens, 'making a universal clatter of iron on the pavement.'

If like Jane Austen you enjoy country walks, you'll find that the ladies' boots currently in fashion are impractical. In Austen's unfinished novel *The Watsons*, when Lord Osborne discovers that Emma Watson has been confined indoors on a fine day by the muddiness of the paths, he comments: "You should wear half-boots... Nothing sets off a neat ankle more than a half-boot; nankeen, galoshed with black, looks very well. Do not you like half-boots?" Emma replies: "Yes; but unless they are so stout as to injure their beauty, they are not fit for country walking".

Because ladies' clothing is so insubstantial, you'll want a large muff (ostrich feather, fur or swansdown), fur tippet or 'bosom-friend' for warmth. The 'bosom-friend', which made its first appearance in the winter of 1791, adorned 'the snowy bosoms of the proudest beauties' and was even worn at court, according to the *Gentleman's Magazine* (November 1792). A 'bosom-friend' is 'an oblong piece of fur doubled square'; place it under your neckerchief when you leave a warm room to go out into the cold.

The summer of 1801 was so unseasonably chilly that Parson Woodforde, who seems to have kept a fatherly eye on his lady visitors' clothing, recorded on 11 July: 'It was so very cold to day [*sic*] that we had a fire – Mrs Custance also felt the cold so much that she wore a fur Tippett [*sic*], a bosom friend & a Muff and a Winter Cloke [*sic*]'.

Umbrellas are essential to protect one's clothes and bonnet from the rain even if you are only walking a short distance. Mrs Allen in *Northanger Abbey* said that umbrellas are 'disagreeable things to carry. I would much rather take a chair'. During the summer a parasol made from sarcenet will shade your face from the sun; a pale complexion is far more elegant than a tan. In *Pride and Prejudice*, Miss Bingley meanly tells Mr Darcy that she thinks Elizabeth Bennet's skin has grown 'brown and coarse!'

Dresses no longer have pockets, so you'll carry a little silk or velvet reticule or ridicule (bag) for your purse, handkerchief, or smelling salts. In *Emma*, Mrs Elton tucks a letter into her 'purple and gold reticule'. You can knit or net your own purse at home. When going shopping, some immodest young ladies hide their purse in their bosom: a treat for any watching gentlemen.

In 1806 reticules fell from fashion and ladies suffering from a streaming cold had nowhere to hide a handkerchief. A writer in *La Belle Assemblée* (December 1806) lamented that gentlemen were now tasked with looking after ladies' snotty handkerchiefs: 'Tender lovers who fancied that they were sighing for a divinity, could no longer disguise the truth from themselves… They all had proofs of it in their hands. It was no longer Flora or Hebe, but plain Mary, or Sarah, attacked with a nasal or pulmonary catarrh.'

MACARONIS AND DANDIES

The days of the 'macaronis' with their towering headdresses, nosegays, satin waistcoats, gaily coloured satin coats with full skirts, tightly cut knee breeches, and diamond shoe buckles are long gone. Macaronis became an endangered species during the 1770s. Coats of plain broadcloth replaced silk frock coats and the skirts were cut away to form a 'morning coat' or riding coat with tails, more practical for riding horses. Lace shirt ruffles disappeared and simple wristbands worn instead.

Francis Grose's *Classical Dictionary of the Vulgar Tongue* (1785) defined 'dandy-prat' as an 'insignificant or trifling fellow', but you are unlikely to hear the term 'dandy' until after 1810. In a letter to Thomas Moore, dated 25 July 1813, Lord Byron wrote: 'The season has closed with a Dandy Ball.'

When Beau Brummell fled to the Continent in 1816 to escape his many creditors, Richard Meyler (of Crawley Hall), whose demands for money precipitated the crisis, earned the sobriquet 'Dick the Dandy-Killer'. But until his ignominious flight, 'Beau' Brummell was the ultimate arbiter of men's fashion, as Captain Gronow recalled: 'All the world watched Brummell to imitate him, and order their clothes of the tradesman who dressed that sublime dandy.' Brummell's tailors were Weston (Old Bond Street), Schweitzer and Davidson in Cork Street (the Prince of Wales's tailors), and Jonathan Meyer in Conduit Street.

For morning dress Brummell wore a beautifully cut blue morning coat with brass buttons, a light or buff coloured waistcoat, buckskins, crisply starched cravat and top-boots. *Ackermann's Repository* for April 1809 reported that 'dark blue, olive, and bottle green' coats with 'silver and gilt basket buttons' were fashionable for dress and morning coats. On the morning of her marriage to George Wickham, flighty Lydia Bennet 'longed to know whether he would be married in his blue coat.'

Coats are cut to fit like a second skin, so your servant will help you haul on your coat. The sleeves are so tight you'll find it difficult to move your arms. An anonymous friend of writer George ('Grantley') Berkeley recalled that Brummell's morning coat 'fitted to a hair; there was not a speck of dust or a crease on the cloth.'

London tailors are incredibly skilled and gentlemen expect high standards from them. Colonel Henry Hervey-Aston (of Aston Hall, Cheshire) always ordered 30 coats at a time from his tailors, and if they did not all fit exactly 'he used to kick them out of the room,' according to George Elers. (Colonel Aston was killed in 1798 in a notorious duel over a trifling misunderstanding with a fellow officer in the East Indies).

If Brummell takes exception to your outfit, he'll make a cutting comment, no matter how exalted your rank. The poet Thomas Moore recalled that one day, the Prince of Wales was so mortified when the Beau 'did not like the cut of his coat' that he 'began to blubber.' In 1800 Moore was promised an introduction to the Prince of Wales, who had given permission for him to dedicate his *Odes of Anacreon* to his Royal Highness. But Moore's coat was too shabby for meeting

Royalty, so he 'got a coat made up in six hours' by his tailor: 'I got it on an economical plan, by giving two guineas and an *old coat*, whereas the usual price of a new coat here is four pounds.' The young Irishman was delighted to meet the Prince, 'He is beyond doubt a man of very fascinating manners.'

A full-length box coat with many shoulder capes will protect you from the weather when driving your carriage. *Northanger Abbey*'s Catherine Morland is bowled over by Henry Tilney's appearance when he takes her for a drive, 'His hat sat so well, and the innumerable capes of his greatcoat looked so becomingly important!'

BUCKSKINS AND 'UNMENTIONABLES'

Breeches are made from leather (buckskin), velvet, wool, silk or cotton, depending on the occasion. Velvet or silk breeches are worn for best. You'll find that leather breeches are most practical for going hunting, but most men don them for everyday wear.

Breeches (also known as 'inexpressibles' or 'unmentionables') are cut to fit precisely, so putting on a brand new pair is a daunting task. Robert Southey recalled that it was 'a good half-hour's work to get them on first time', and even when assisted by his breeches-maker he 'had to use all his strength... to force himself into them.'

When George Elers was a schoolboy, he had a new pair of 'unmentionables' for his holidays, as he recalled in his *Memoirs*: 'I had the greatest difficulty getting into [*them*] – a feat I accomplished not without assistance. Our servant, I recollect, fairly lifted me off the ground in the operation. And then the buttoning of them, and, when once buttoned, the difficulty of undoing!' It can be disastrous to get caught out in the rain while wearing leather breeches; you'll practically have to peel them off when wet.

Don't use the term 'small-clothes' for your breeches unless you wish to be thought whimsical and effeminate. The critic of the *Anti-Jacobin Review* (December 1813) was outraged when this word appeared in a biography of raconteur John Horne Tooke: 'His breeches he calls *small-clothes* – the first time we have seen this bastard term... in print... this is an age of affectation – even our fish-women, and milkmaids, affect to blush at the only word which can express this part of a man's dress, and lisp *small-clothes*, with as many airs as a would-be woman of fashion is accustomed to display.'

When you see children out and about with their nursery maid, some little 'girls' are actually male. Boys are dressed in girls' clothing in their early years, then 'breeched' when they are a few years old. In a letter to Cassandra (5 September 1796), Jane Austen wrote: 'Little Edward [*her nephew*] was breeched yesterday for good and all, and was whipped into the bargain.'

George Elers recalled in his *Memoirs*: 'My little brother Ned was a fine little fellow in petticoats; large blue eyes, a fine fair skin, and light straight hair, very saucy and very passionate, very bold and daring – in short, a boy that any mother might well be proud of.'

For evening wear, modish men like Brummell wear a blue coat and white waistcoat, striped silk stockings, pantaloons and hessian boots. Pantaloons first became fashionable in the 1790s. They are longer than breeches; when dressing, button them closely to the ankle before pulling on your hessians. Knee breeches are still worn for full dress. Pantaloons are knitted; they fit the wearer extremely closely and leave little to ladies' imaginations. John Beresford dubbed over-tight pantaloons as one of his *Miseries of Human Life*: 'A pair of pantaloons so constructed with what the taylors [*sic*] call *the stride*, as to limit you to three or four inches per step.'

Beau Brummell and his tailor Mr Meyer are both credited with inventing men's trousers: the Beau was the first person to wear them, according to his biographer Captain Jesse. Trousers are more loose fitting than pantaloons, and fasten with buttons and loops. They are not considered suitable evening wear at some select establishments, as we shall see later.

The practical design of men's clothing suits the 'bucks' who keep themselves fit by boxing, fencing, riding and hunting. They are more carelessly dressed than men of fashion, and are sometimes mistaken for their groom or coachman. In *Northanger Abbey*, impudent John Thorpe, a 'stout young man… seemed fearful of being too handsome, unless he wore the dress of a groom.'

MEN'S LINEN

Men wear linen or cotton drawers under their breeches. Cotton, which is lightweight and easy to wash, has become very popular and men's 'Drawers, stockings, breeches, pantaloons, neck-cloths, vests, and often even shirts' are made from cotton, as John Wilkes noted in the *Encyclopedia Londinensis* (1810).

Gentlemen should take care with their personal hygiene, unless they wish to disgust their female friends. You can often smell a typical country gentleman from ten paces away because his boots reek of horse muck and cheap blacking. When out walking, the stink of stale sweat will inform you that people do not change their personal linen very frequently. This is because of the several weeks' wait until the next 'great wash'; one needs many pairs of shirts, drawers, etc to have enough for a whole month or more.

Mr Brummell has made filthiness unfashionable, although few emulate the five hours he spends washing, bathing and getting dressed each day. In his *Life of George Brummell* (1844), Captain Jesse wrote that the *only* extreme part of the Beau's appearance was his 'extreme cleanliness and neatness,' owing to 'very fine linen, plenty of it, and country washing.'

A large supply of linen is required to follow Brummell's gospel of absolute cleanliness. According to Prince Pückler-Muskau, each week you will need at least 20 shirts, 24 pocket handkerchiefs, nine or 10 pairs of 'summer trowsers, 30 neckerchiefs (cravats), a dozen waistcoats, and stockings as needed.'

After you have put on your shirt, your valet will bring a snow-white muslin or silk cravat (neck-cloth) to tie around your neck. Captain Gronow explained 'It was the fashion to wear a deep, stiff white cravat, which prevented you from seeing your boots while standing.' You and your valet may need several attempts to create an elegant style like the 'Oriental' or 'Mathematical'. Starch will help you achieve a crisp turnout.

Men rely on their female relatives to make their cravats and shirts. In a letter to her niece Fanny Knight, Jane Austen wrote: 'I have contributed the marking to Uncle H's [*Henry's*] shirts, and now they are the complete memorial of the tender regard of many.' In *Mansfield Park*, Fanny Price busily plied her needle to get her brother Sam's linen ready for his voyage.

Some men wear flannel under-waistcoats next to their skin for warmth and comfort; a fresh linen shirt can feel icy-cold when you first put it on. *Sense and Sensibility's* Marianne Dashwood mocks 35-year-old Colonel Brandon (named as a possible suitor) after he mentions flannel waistcoats, which she feels are associated with 'aches, cramps, rheumatisms, and every species of ailment that can afflict the old and the feeble.'

Tight-laced stays ('riding belts' or 'Cumberland corsets') are worn by those beyond the first flush of youth, military men who want to stand tall, and corpulent gentlemen such as the Prince of Wales. Puny gentlemen add artificial padding to their chests and calves so that they look muscular.

Brummell was never extreme in his dress, but the term 'dandy' has become synonymous with tightly-laced 'exquisites':

'The Dandy' (*Sporting Magazine*, December 1818)

Why here comes a Dandy – describe me who can, –
An exhibit of all that's conceited in man.
If to please be the object of every man's care,
He shews his intent, by contempt of the fair,
If t'excel be the object of every man's boast,
His ambition appears – in the cut of his coat.
But what are the arts by which Dandies must rise?
A pair of shirt collars of marvellous size...
A cravat so stiffen'd, so standing, with starch,
That the bedpost must help you to give it an arch –
A coat, with a collar of thirty-six inches,
A waist, which the ribs of a skeleton pinches,
Well-rounded lapels, and a chest so well-padded,
You'd almost suspect that a breast might be added.

These 'exquisites', with their painted faces, are ridiculed for wearing stays so tightly laced that they cannot bend over like ordinary mortals if they drop a scented handkerchief: 'It is found remarkably convenient in such a case for the exquisite to carry a cane or stick with a hook at the end, as he might thereby fish up anything he unfortunately drops, without breaking his back, or exciting the pity or risibility of the spectators'. (*Kilmarnock Mirror*, January 1819).

Taking care of one's appearance does not preclude other interests. Sir Lumley Skeffington, a 'consummate old fop' according to Captain Gronow, can easily be recognised by his painted face and overpowering smell of perfume. He is very popular with the ladies, however, and well-known for his literary works and patronage of the theatre.

BEAVERS AND BOOTS

A 'round' beaver hat with a brim is worn for morning wear and 'undress'. For full dress you'll need a *chapeau bras* or 'cocked hat': a two-cornered formal hat shaped like a half-moon which you tuck under your arm when at a ball. Like the fair sex, you should wear white gloves when dancing; leather gloves are best for riding.

Indoors you'll wear leather shoes fastened with ribbons or shoestrings of leather or whipcord; shoe buckles fell out of fashion in the last century. Boots with white tops are *de rigeur* when walking or riding; the best bootmakers are Hoby's of Bond Street, London. Your boots should be brilliantly polished, and gentlemen are willing to pay enormous wages to a valet who possesses the secret of turning out his master in grand style.

According to Captain Gronow, one day a young gentleman approached Brummell and timorously asked him where he got the blacking for his boots? '"Ah!" replied Brummell, gazing complacently at his footwear, "My blacking positively ruins me. I will tell you inconfidence; it is made with the finest champagne!"'

To complete your outfit, you'll need a pocket watch and some jewellery – perhaps a ring containing a lock of hair from a loved one. In *Sense and Sensibility*, Edward Ferrars wears a ring with Lucy

Steele's hair, but Elinor Dashwood mistakenly thinks it is her own hair, somehow acquired by some 'theft or contrivance' unknown to her. Wearing a sword in public is no longer polite unless you are a military man or a physician, although it is still required for court dress.

Many men of fashion carry a gold-topped walking cane for exploring the city, and an expensive toothpick-case or snuffbox in their pocket. Snuff-taking (breathing in a pinch of special tobacco), originally a French fashion, was first made popular in England by Queen Charlotte, wife of George III. On 3 March 1789, Parson Woodforde paid 1s 5d for half a pound (225g) of tobacco and 'one pennyworth of Scotch snuff' from his local shopkeeper in Norfolk.

Lord Petersham (later 4th Earl of Harrington), a noted dandy, reputedly has a different snuffbox for every day of the year. Petersham, a connoisseur of snuff (and tea), likes to experiment and create his own mixtures. He carefully matches his snuffboxes to his apparel, and once commented that a light blue Sèvres box he was using was a 'nice summer box, but would not do for winter wear.' The Prince Regent always carries a snuffbox, to keep in with the current fashion, but does not really like taking snuff. He has perfected a special manner of appearing to inhale it without actually allowing any to enter his nose. Fribourg & Pontet on Pall Mall supply the Royal family with snuff, including the Prince. Rival firm Fribourg & Treyer on the Haymarket sell imported snuff to the court.

Snuff-takers have an inelegant habit of sneezing drips of brown goo, and their faces and clothes become covered in powdered snuff. Jane Austen did not approve of this dirty habit. After a visit to some new acquaintances in London, the D'Entraigues, she wrote to Cassandra (25 April 1811): 'I see nothing to dislike in them but their taking quantities of snuff.'

CHAPTER 4

Money Matters

*'Female economy will do a great deal... but it cannot turn
a small income into a large one.'*
(Jane Austen, *The Watsons,* composed circa 1804)

As you become better acquainted with English life, you will be struck
by its highly stratified nature – not only the class system, but also
within families. Why is an eldest son the cosseted darling of the
family? Why is the master of a household so 'courted' by his relatives
and dependents? The answer lies in the laws of 'primogeniture'.

ELDEST SONS AND ENTAILS
The upper classes and the landed gentry live on the income from their
estates, or the interest from investments such as government 'consols'.
It's considered vital to transmit a family's estate from one generation
to the next without splitting it up. The eldest son is the primary heir to
his father's property. When he marries or succeeds to the estate, he
must take steps to ensure that his eldest son, too, will inherit the estate
as intact as possible.

When an eldest son marries, a legal settlement is drawn up so that
his future unborn son will inherit the estate in turn. An heir is unable
to alienate the estate, e.g. by selling or mortgaging it, without
undergoing a very costly legal process.

When Sir Walter Elliot gets into debt in Austen's *Persuasion*, 'There
was only a small amount of the estate that Sir Walter could dispose of,
but had every acre been alienable, it would have made no difference.
He had condescended to mortgage as far as he had the power, but he

would never condescend to sell. No; he would never disgrace his name so far. The Kellynch estate should be transmitted whole and entire, as he had received it.'

If a couple have no male heir, just daughters, and the estate is 'entailed', when the father dies it passes to the nearest male heir in the family tree. If there is no entail the couple's daughters share the estate equally. In *Pride and Prejudice*, the entail on the Longbourn estate has important consequences for the Bennet girls. 'When first Mr Bennet had married, economy was held to be perfectly useless; for, of course, they would have a son. This son would join in cutting off the entail as soon as he should be of age, and the widow and younger children would by that means be provided for.' The lack of a male heir means that Mrs Bennet and her daughters will have little money when Mr Bennet dies because the Longbourn estate will descend to the heir, the obsequious Mr Collins. As Mr Bennet says: "When I am dead, Mr Collins 'may turn you all out of this house as soon as he pleases."

Primogeniture has unfortunate consequences for an eldest son's siblings. His younger brothers must find themselves a profession: the army or navy, the church, a government sinecure, the law, or (if there is no alternative) commerce, which is not considered genteel.

An eldest son is expected to make a good match – an heiress with a large fortune or, better still, estates to add to his own will fit the bill nicely. Because the male heir is the family's hope for the future, eldest sons like Tom Bertram in *Mansfield Park* are often spoilt and extravagant, 'born only for expense and enjoyment.' He is a prime catch for worldly females on the lookout for a husband. Mary Crawford 'had felt an early presentiment that she *should* like the eldest best. She knew it was her way.'

But if you are a *younger* son, then mothers whose daughters who are 'out' will do their utmost to keep you away from them. As *Pride and Prejudice's* Colonel Fitzwilliam says: 'Younger sons cannot marry where they like… Our habits of expense make us too dependent, and there are not many in my rank of life who can afford to marry without some attention to money.' As Elizabeth Bennet says, younger sons 'very often… like women of fortune.'

To counter the unfairness of primogeniture, the second son of a marriage is sometimes left money or land by his maternal relations. In *Mansfield Park,* Mary Crawford is surprised and alarmed when she hears that Edmund Bertram plans to earn his living as a clergyman, 'There is generally an uncle or a grandfather to leave a fortune to the second son.'

The upper classes expect their daughters, too, to marry a husband with a large estate. In 1774 two great English families were united when Lady Georgiana Spencer married the fabulously wealthy William Cavendish, Duke of Devonshire. The Duke and Duchess gave their eldest daughter, Georgiana, a lavish first London season and in 1801 she married Lord Morpeth, the Earl of Carlisle's eldest son. The Duke of Devonshire settled £30,000 on his daughter and gave her £1,500 pin money annually.

In *Pride and Prejudice*, Mr Darcy's cousin Miss de Bourgh is destined to have a 'very large fortune, and it is believed that she and her cousin will unite the two estates,' according to George Wickham.

Marriage is the easiest way for the aspiring middle classes to ascend the social scale. An heiress is a desirable match for a hard-up aristocrat even if her fortune derives from trade or commerce – banking, brewing, or agriculture. A writer in the *Atheneum* (1 December 1817) commented that assemblies, balls and operas were types of:

> Public markets, where faces are put up for sale, and where dealers in matrimony go to make purchases. The goods are therefore very properly exposed as much as possible... Here Lombard Street and St James's meet to transact compacts of conveniency [*sic*]. The old jewels want new setting, so an impoverished title and plebeian plum enter into a treaty; a balance is struck with rent-rolls and family trees... and the coronet unites its fate with the sugar hogshead.

Young ladies put their wares on show – a pretty face, musical skills, or witty repartee – while 'the lords of creation, who had probably spent the morning at Tattersall's strut up and down the room, examine paces and points, and at length select their purchase.'

Similarly, a young middle class man whose family fortune was founded in trade but who is now wealthy enough to purchase an estate and become one of the landed gentry, like *Pride and Prejudice*'s Mr Bingley, is a most eligible match for a gentleman's daughter – he 'must be in want of a wife.'

However, anyone who marries too far below their station risks opprobrium. When *Pride and Prejudice*'s Lady Catherine de Bourgh hears rumours that Darcy will marry Elizabeth Bennet she is outraged by her seeming presumption: 'A young woman of inferior birth, of no importance in the world, and wholly unallied to the family!' If Elizabeth marries Darcy: 'You will be censured, slighted, and despised, by everyone connected with him. Your alliance will be a disgrace.'

A middle class son or daughter who marries to disoblige their parents also runs the risk of being disinherited or becoming a social outcast, cut off from their family. In *Emma*, 'Miss Churchill, of a great Yorkshire family... with the full command of her own fortune' marries Captain Weston without one, to her family's intense mortification, so her brother and his wife 'threw her off with due decorum.'

A gentleman who marries an heiress sometimes adds her family name to his as part of the marriage settlement. Cecilia Beverley, the heroine of Fanny Burney's *Cecilia, or Memoirs of an Heiress* has a fortune of £10,000. The plot of the novel hinges on her father's will: Cecilia cannot access her fortune until she is 21, and when she marries she must keep the Beverley name.

THE RIGHT CONNECTIONS
The more far-sighted members of the upper classes and nobility augment their wealth by improving their estates and exploiting mineral resources (e.g. coal). The more money you have, the more land and property you can buy – and the more prosperous your children will be.

The right social connections are vital for sons destined for a career in high life. After private tuition at home, they'll go to a school such as Eton or Harrow. A spell at Oxford or Cambridge (the only two universities in England at present) is next. Many scholars do not bother to take their degree – it's the social mix that is important. A university education is essential, too, if your sons are destined for a career in the church.

A 'Grand Tour' of Europe is traditionally the accepted way of rounding off your sons' education. The war with France made travelling there difficult, so in the late 1780s, Jane Austen's brother Edward was sent by his adopted parents, the Knights, to Dresden and Rome for his grand tour.

A career in politics or public office can prove extremely lucrative. When your son has come of age (earlier, if possible) a seat in the House of Commons should set him up for life. Parliamentary seats are on sale to the highest bidder; the great county families often divide up the available seats in their shire between them. Families such as the Grosvenors of Eaton Hall, Cheshire, spend tens of thousands of pounds 'treating' their voters at election times to ensure that their candidate wins. General Thomas Grosvenor, the Earl's brother, was MP for Chester for three decades.

The army is a very fashionable career for younger sons of aristocrats. It can cost over a thousand pounds to buy a commission, so the nobility has the pick of the most senior army ranks. Lower ranks, for example an ensigncy or cornetcy, are slightly more affordable, but are still a few hundred pounds.

In 1797 'Beau' Brummell bought a cornetcy in the Prince of Wales' regiment, the 10th Hussars, after coming into some money when his father died. He 'soon became the pet of the officers... and was invited, as a matter of course, into whatever society the Prince of Wales frequented.'

Young ladies adore men in uniform, as *Pride and Prejudice*'s Mrs Bennet says: 'I remember the time when I liked a red coat myself very well... and if a smart young colonel, with five or six thousand a year, should want one of my girls, I should not say nay to him.'

As an army commission is so expensive, the navy is a more likely career option for middle class lads, especially if they have a patron willing to help. Jane Austen's brothers Francis (Frank) and Charles both saw active service, and their promotions were aided by Admiral Gambier, one of the Lords of the Admiralty. Frank ended his career as an Admiral of the Fleet; Charles eventually became a Rear-Admiral. In Austen's *Mansfield Park*, Fanny Price's brother William is made second lieutenant of HMS *Thrush* after her suitor Henry Crawford asks his uncle, an Admiral, to recommend him for promotion.

A successful capture of an enemy ship can haul in riches for a naval officer. In *Persuasion*, snobby Sir Walter Elliot complains that the navy is the 'means of bringing persons of obscure birth into undue distinction.' The baronet gives Captain Wentworth, who had 'no fortune', a very cold reception when he becomes engaged to his daughter Anne, and her friend Lady Russell persuades her to end the engagement. When the captain proposes a second time to Anne some years later, Sir Walter no longer objects: 'Captain Wentworth, with five-and-twenty thousand pounds, and as high in his profession as merit and activity could place him, was... now esteemed quite worthy to address the daughter of a foolish, spendthrift baronet.'

The Church is another good career choice for upper and middle class sons, providing they can obtain a decent living; many curates are as poor as church mice. It helps if you are intimately acquainted with someone like *Pride and Prejudice*'s Mr Darcy who has 'considerable patronage' in the church. The obnoxious Mr Collins has 'a good house and very sufficient income' at Hunsford parsonage thanks to Lady Catherine de Bourgh, to whom he is eternally grateful.

The sons of the middle classes can choose from a huge range of careers: manufacturer, physician, surgeon, apothecary, commercial traveller, lawyer, merchant, tradesman, etc. Daniel Vawdrey (1771–1844) of Middlewich trained as a barrister, and served five years as an articled clerk with a firm of Manchester solicitors. But when his father died in 1801, he became wealthy enough to retire from the law and live as a country gentleman.

If you or your family are genteel but not wealthy you need rich or influential family friends and patrons to help further your career. Jane Austen's father, George, had his fees at Tonbridge School paid by his well-off Uncle Francis of Sevenoaks. This in turn enabled George to take advantage of a free scholarship available to ex-Tonbridge boys at St John's College, Oxford. He later became a Fellow of the College.

In the 1760s, when George wanted to marry Cassandra Leigh, they needed an income and family connections came to the rescue here, too. George Austen's living at Steventon was in the gift of his wealthy relation, Thomas Knight, and George's other living at nearby Deane was bought for him by his Uncle Francis.

George Austen's main income was from tithes: the two livings brought in roughly £200 p.a. at that date. George's income was augmented by produce from his farms, but this was not enough for the rector's growing family, and he took in boy pupils to supplement his income.

Over three decades later, when the Austen family was preparing to move to Bath, Jane wrote to Cassandra (3 January 1801): 'My father is doing all in his power to increase his income, by raising his tithes, etc., and I do not despair of getting very nearly six hundred a year.'

George could not afford to pay for his sons James and Henry to attend university. However, Mrs Austen (Cassandra Leigh) was related to the Perrot family (named Leigh-Perrot after 1751 when James Leigh inherited an estate from his relative Thomas Perrot) and through them to Sir Thomas White, founder of St John's College, Oxford. James and Henry were granted 'founder's kin' scholarships at St John's, owing to their mother's connection with Sir Thomas White.

James, the eldest, went to Oxford in 1779, when he was only 14 years old. James took over the duties of the Steventon living when his father retired. Henry originally intended to take orders but joined the Oxford militia, before commencing an ill-fated spell as a banker. After his banking business failed, he too became a clergyman.

Opportunities for Roman Catholics are limited owing to the Test Acts. Catholics cannot study at university or take public office. (The Book of Common Prayer still includes a special service giving thanks for the nation's deliverance from the Gunpowder Plot by rogue Catholics in 1605). Until 1793, when the law was relaxed, Roman Catholics could not study law, either. The mother of Thomas Moore (author of *Lalla Rookh*) was keen for him to study law, and luckily the restrictions were lifted just at the right time; Thomas enrolled at Trinity College, Dublin in 1794.

WIVES AND DAUGHTERS

It's a man's world. A husband and wife are 'one person' in the eyes of the law. A woman's property becomes her husband's when she marries. A wife has little protection in law if her husband wastes all her property and fortune, or treats her badly. So when a daughter marries, a wise parent settles some money or property exclusively on her and her children, just in case.

When Parson Woodforde's niece, Jane Pounsett, married the Rev Frederick Grove in Somerset in 1798, he was very upset to hear that her marriage settlement is 'a very bad one & a very cunning one for in case she dies without Issue, everything whatever goes to Grove immediately on her demise.' When Jane's mother, Mrs Pounsett, died that December, she left a will bequeathing as much of her estate as possible to her sister and family so that her son-in-law, who allegedly treated her very unkindly, did not get all *her* property as well.

There are some 'advantages' to the marriage laws. A spendthrift wife who has run up debts, for example, for clothes and jewels, is not responsible for paying her creditors – her husband must settle them. Georgiana, Duchess of Devonshire was terrified that her husband would find out the true extent of her gambling debts after he thought he had already paid them.

When a marriage settlement is drawn up for the heir to an estate, arrangements are made (for example by mortgaging the estate) so that his wife will have a regular income, and portions are set aside for the heir's siblings when they come of age, or get married.

In *Pride and Prejudice*, 'Five thousand pounds was settled by marriage articles on Mrs Bennet and the children. But in what proportions it should be divided amongst the latter depended on the will of the parents'. Each Bennet girl 'unhappily' only has a small 'portion', as Mr Collins reminds Elizabeth when he proposes to her.

When giddy Lydia Bennet marries George Wickham, Mr Bennet guarantees Lydia an equal share of the £5,000 for her marriage settlement, plus an annual income of £100 during his lifetime (and £50 yearly after his death).

A widow is entitled to a 'dower' – one-third of her late husband's freehold land – during her lifetime. It's customary for the widow to move out of the family seat and retire to a dower house on the estate. When Thomas Knight died (Jane Austen's brother Edward's adopted father), he left his estates to his wife for her lifetime. But three years after his death, Mrs Knight handed them over to their adopted son, first reserving an income of £2,000 for herself. She moved out of the manor house at Godmersham Park so that Edward, his wife and growing family could move in.

When a couple become engaged, their property is already 'tied up'; the lady's property is deemed to belong to her fiancé. Cassandra Austen became engaged to young clergyman Thomas Fowle in 1795, but they could not afford to marry immediately. Fortunately, as it seemed, his relative Lord Craven offered him a place as chaplain to his regiment when he went out to the West Indies. Two years later, news reached the Austen family that Thomas had died from yellow fever. Lord Craven later commented that if he had known that Thomas was engaged, he would never have taken him to such a notorious fever spot. Thomas had made a will in Cassandra's favour and when he died in the West Indies, she received a bequest of £1,000 from him, which gave her an income of her own. She never married.

Because most women are dependent on their husband or male relatives, it is bad form for a young man to break off an engagement. A jilted girl is deprived of her future provision for life (or more accurately, for her husband's lifetime). A young lady whose engagement has been broken by a gentleman has been publicly rejected, so she may never find another suitor. Edward Ferrars (*Sense and Sensibility*) feels he cannot end his engagement to Lucy Steele, who he believes is 'a well-disposed, good-hearted girl, and thoroughly attached to himself', even though he has fallen in love with Elinor Dashwood and deeply regrets his engagement.

Some women sue their former lovers for breach of promise to claim damages for their blighted future prospects. *The Sporting Magazine* (March 1810) reported a breach of promise case. Mr Flowers, a ribbon manufacturer in Cheapside, was a widower with 'many children'. He wrote several love letters to Miss Mary Willis, 'the daughter of a very respectable man in the same trade.' In one letter, dated October 1804, he wrote: 'I long to see you at the head of my table – to see you my wife; that is the only hope that can make life desirable.' But Flowers married another lady, and they had a child. Miss Willis won £500 damages (worth approximately £38,000 in 2013) even though she waited some years before bringing the case, perhaps owing to the 'shame and pain which a respectable female felt in becoming… an object in the public eye.'

If your marriage is not 'happy ever after' because of your partner's adultery or cruelty, you may consider a separation or divorce in spite of the scandal. But only well-off people can afford a separation via the ecclesiastical courts or a costly divorce by Act of Parliament.

A husband has the right to chastise his wife, so long as he does not overdo it, and can even stop her going out. Legally he has sole custody of his wife's children, and if the couple divorce or separate he can stop her seeing them altogether. In polite society, a wife is also expected to turn a blind eye to her husband's infidelities, unless they become so blatant that there is a public scandal. Lord and Lady Nelson were formally separated in early 1801 owing to Nelson's infatuation with Emma, Lady Hamilton.

Upper class married ladies often indulge in affairs. This is not frowned on so long as they are discreet, and have already provided their husband with a legitimate heir or two. If a husband discovers that his wife has been unfaithful, he may challenge her lover to a duel, or sue him for damages – a 'crim. con.' or 'criminal conversation' case. Duels and 'crim. con.' cases are regular fodder for newspapers such as the *Morning Post*.

One of the biggest scandals of the day is the Prince of Wales's disastrous love life. He has had a succession of mistresses (including Lady Jersey, patroness of Almack's Assembly Rooms), and in 1785 he contracted an illegal 'marriage' to a Roman Catholic widow, Mrs Fitzherbert. Ten years later the Prince married the tactless and indiscreet Princess Caroline of Brunswick (1768–1821) purely to pay off his vast debts. Although the couple produced an heir to the throne, Princess Charlotte, they soon began living separately.

The Prince's infidelities and the ungallant way he treats his wife are common knowledge amongst all classes and Princess Caroline has many supporters among the public (Jane Austen among them), despite her many character flaws.

FASHIONABLE ACCOMPLISHMENTS

Girls' education prepares them for the marriage 'market' and their future lives as wives and mothers. They must know how to read and write and 'cast up accounts' so that they can run a household. Girls (and boys) are brought up to respect their parents and be truthful, religious, and obedient.

Girls are usually taught at home at first, then sent either to a 'seminary... where young ladies for enormous pay might be screwed out of health and into vanity', or alternatively to a 'real, honest, old-fashioned boarding school', like Mrs Goddard's establishment in *Emma*: 'where a reasonable quantity of accomplishments were sold at a reasonable price, and where girls might be sent to be out of the way, and scramble themselves into a little education, without any danger of coming back prodigies.' 'Accomplishments' include letter writing, painting and drawing, correct deportment, needlework, languages, the use of 'the globes', and so on.

Mary Russell Mitford, a precocious Hampshire child, learned to read by the age of three. When she was 11 years old she went to a school run by a French émigré at 22 Hans Place, Chelsea (not far from Sloane Street, where Jane Austen's brother Henry lived several years later). Mitford learned French, history, geography, a little science, Italian, music, dancing and drawing. She studied Latin, too, after a tussle with her parents, who thought it an unnecessary accomplishment for a female.

Another contemporary of Jane Austen, Frances Winckley (who later married Sir John Shelley), went to school in Twickenham for two years when she was about eight years old. After her father's death she stayed at her mother's house in Bath and was taught by a governess. When Frances was 15 she went to a very expensive London school, run by Mrs Olier, so that she could have the benefit of the best masters.

Music is considered an ideal accomplishment for young ladies and Jane Austen's brother Henry recalled that when at Chawton, she 'practised [*the pianoforte*] daily, chiefly before breakfast.' The fair sex are much in demand at dinner parties if they can play and sing well, like *Emma*'s Jane Fairfax.

So a typical girl's 'fashionable education' is similar to that of Lady Honoria Pemberton in Fanny Burney's *Cecilia*: 'Her proficiency had been equal to what fashion made requisite; she sung a little, played the harpsichord a little, painted a little, worked [*her needle*] a little, and danced a great deal.'

MONEY AND THE SINGLE WOMAN

A single gentlewoman with no income of her own is totally dependent on her parents and after their death, on any male relatives she possesses. If they are married she may have to 'earn her keep' looking after their children or acting as a domestic drudge. 'Single women have a dreadful propensity for being poor, which is one very strong argument in favour of matrimony,' Jane wrote to one of her favourite nieces, Fanny Knight, who was dithering over a potential suitor.

Simple economics pushes some women into marriage even if their future husband is not exactly the man of their dreams. In *Pride and Prejudice*, Elizabeth Bennet's homely friend Charlotte Lucas knows that she *must* find a husband. Marriage is 'the only honourable provision for well-educated women of small fortune, and, however uncertain of giving happiness, must be their pleasantest preservative from want.' Elizabeth is horrified by Charlotte's betrothal to Mr Collins, but Charlotte is being practical. Her engagement not only ensures her a secure future but also helps her family because they will no longer have to support her. The rest of her family are 'overjoyed', and her younger sisters 'formed hopes of *coming out* a year or two sooner than they might otherwise have done; and the boys were relieved from their apprehension of Charlotte's dying an old maid.'

Writing is one of the few genteel occupations open to single middle class women like Jane Austen, Harriet Martineau and the widowed Mary Shelley. Austen's books turned a modest but welcome profit, even though they were published at her own expense. By the summer of 1813 she had received £110 for the copyright of *Pride and Prejudice*, plus another £140 profit from *Sense and Sensibility* (which had sold out). She took great pleasure in her literary earnings. 'I have now, therefore, written myself into £250, which only makes me long for more,' she wrote to her brother Frank. (The sum of £250 is roughly £15,000 in modern terms).

A post as a governess is considered respectable, although middle class ladies seeking paid employment like Jane Fairfax in *Emma* are viewed as quitting the social sphere they grew up in. Miss Fairfax does not want a place with a rich family because: 'my mortifications, I think, would only be the greater. I should suffer more from comparison. A gentleman's family is all that I should condition for.'

But the 'governess trade' is a far more attractive proposition than destitution or prostitution – the last resort for poor women. Like Jane Austen and her sister, clergyman's daughter Agnes Porter (1750–1814) had very little to live on after her father's death. Fortunately she obtained the position of governess to the 2nd Earl of Ilchester's family at their Somerset home, and served them for two decades.

Jane Austen herself faced the prospect of being a poor old maid if she could not find a suitable husband. Little is known for certain about her love life. Her niece Caroline was told by Cassandra that in about 1801 Jane met a young man during a trip to the seaside (perhaps Sidmouth). He 'seemed greatly attracted' to her and had 'fallen in love.' But Jane's un-named suitor died suddenly. Caroline added that Cassandra thought that 'he was worthy of her sister' and that he 'would have been a successful suitor.'

The following year, according to Caroline, Jane accepted a proposal of marriage from a family friend, the highly eligible Harris Bigg-Wither. But upon thinking it over, 'having accepted him she found she was miserable,' and she broke off the engagement the next morning. Jane was then about 27 years old. She must have known that she was throwing away a comfortable future, and was unlikely to get another offer. But as she later wrote to her niece Fanny Knight: 'Nothing can be compared to the misery of being bound *without* love – bound to one, and preferring another.' Jane preferred to risk a bleak old age as a poor old maid rather than marry a man she did not love.

Her rich and single fictional heroine Emma Woodhouse jokes that she has no fear of becoming an old maid like Miss Bates in *Emma*: 'It is poverty only which makes celibacy contemptible to a generous public! A single woman with a very narrow income must be a ridiculous, disagreeable old maid! The proper sport of boys and girls; but a single woman of good fortune is always respectable.'

If you are an old maid but a rich one, never despair of finding a husband at last. The *British Mercury* (13 October 1788) reported the story of a rich spinster in a country village. She was convinced that death was imminent and paid the parish sexton to dig a 'handsome deep grave' ready for her. However, a 'jolly young farmer' attracted by her fortune persuaded her to marry him. As the happy couple were on their way to church, they passed the sexton who was busy digging a large hole for the lady's final resting place as requested. The bride gave the sexton a guinea, and asked him to fill in the hole again – she did not need it after all.

THE SERVANT PROBLEM

A country gentleman with a large income like Mr Darcy, that is £10,000 a year, will spend about one-third of his income on household expenses including food, according to Samuel and Sarah Adams' *The Complete Servant* (1826). Another quarter of his income goes on clothing, children's education, medical fees, personal expenses, entertaining, etc, and about one-eighth on rent, taxes, house repairs and so on.

Servants, liveries, horses and carriages will require another quarter of his income. Liveried servants are a real status symbol. The Duke of Kent (the Regent's brother) employed a hairdresser at his Middlesex cottage *orné*, Castle Hill, solely for dressing and powdering the hair of his liveried servants.

A family with children living on £4–5,000 p.a. needs 11 female and 13 male servants: 'A Housekeeper, Cook, Lady's Maid, Nurse, two House-maids, Laundry-Maid, Still-room Maid, Nursery-maid, Kitchen-maid, and Scullion, with Butler, Valet, House-Steward, Coachman, two Grooms, one assistant ditto, two Footmen, three Gardeners, and a Labourer.' The Adams recommend that a family on a more modest £500 p.a. can afford a 'Cook, House-maid, and Nursery-maid', plus an occasional gardener. In Austen's *Sense and Sensibility*, when Mr Dashwood dies, his widow's income is £500 annually. Her daughter Elinor advises her to sell the horses and carriage, and manage with two maidservants and a manservant. If you own horses you will require a groom and stable boy. When Willoughby offers to give a horse to Marianne Dashwood, her sister Elinor explains that their mother cannot afford this additional expense. She would have to buy 'another [*horse*] for the servant, and keep a servant to ride it... and build a stable.'

According to Mrs William Parkes' *Domestic Duties*, (1825) a valet in London earns about £47 p.a.; a housekeeper in London up to £42, a cook up to £31, and a 'maid of all work' 14 guineas (£14 14s) annually.

Even households on a very narrow income like that of Mrs Price in *Mansfield Park* have servants to cook, serve and clean. When Fanny Price is banished from her adopted home and sent to live with her parents in a 'small house' at Portsmouth, she's met at the door by Rebecca, a 'trollopy-looking maid-servant'. Rebecca is the so-called 'upper servant', and under her is an 'attendant girl' called Sally, of 'inferior appearance': the kitchen is her province. Fanny's mother Mrs Price is convinced that 'of all the Portsmouth servants... her own two were the very worst.'

The 'great wash' is another significant household expense: Dolly Clayton of Lostock Hall in Lancashire paid an expensive seven shillings for 'washing' in January 1777. Some households send away their laundry to be done, which can be very costly; others employ a laundry-maid. When you engage a laundry-maid, make sure that she understands her business thoroughly, or your muslin gowns and household linen will be spoilt. As Mrs Parkes notes: 'Your eyes will quickly tell you if she wash [*sic*] the linen clean, and get up fine muslin tolerably well.'

Parson Woodforde at Weston Longueville employed washerwomen, who usually came to the parsonage every five weeks. Good weather was crucial for this major household event. On 13 November 1792 he noted: 'A most delightful day for drying our Linnen [*sic*] – We having a great Quantity this time – 7 weeks – The two last Weeks we were obliged to put it off.'

Speak civilly to your servants but not too familiarly, or they may become insolent or impertinent. Always ask your servants to leave the room before you discuss any private or personal family business, unless you want all your friends and neighbours to know your most intimate affairs. When Lydia Bennet elopes with George Wickham in *Pride and Prejudice*, her mother keeps to her room in a 'dreadful state'. Mrs Bennet's seclusion is unopposed by Mr and Mrs Gardiner, because 'they knew that she had not prudence enough to hold her tongue before the servants, while they waited at table, and judged it better that *one* only of the household, and the one whom they could most trust, should comprehend all her fears and solicitude on the subject.'

Your female domestics should be clean and tidily dressed in muslin (not lace) caps, cotton and stuff gowns and petticoats, sturdy shawls of demure colours, and straw bonnets when going outdoors. In *Persuasion*, Mrs Musgrove complains that her daughter-in-law Mary's 'nursery-maid... is always upon the gad, and... she is such a fine-dressing lady, that she is enough to ruin any servants she comes near.'

A good master or mistress ensures their servants receive good, plain, plentiful food, and pays their medical expenses if ill. You should permit servants to visit their friends and relations occasionally; Sunday is usually the most convenient day. Fortunately, you are no longer expected to give vails (gratuities) to servants when visiting a private household, as Mrs Parkes says: 'I am happy to find it is a custom growing into disuse, and is actually prohibited in many houses, where the servants would instantly lose their places, if they were known to receive vails.'

Take care to select servants with good references. Unfortunately masters and mistresses often give good references to bad servants, either to get rid of them, or from mistaken compassion. When Jane Bennet becomes engaged to Mr Bingley in *Pride and Prejudice*, her father jokes that: 'You are each of you so complying, that nothing will ever be resolved on; so easy, that every servant will cheat you; and so generous, that you will always exceed your income.'

A servant looking for a new job may be a trickster. In April 1784 at Bapchild in Kent, horse dealer David Thompson fell into the company of a waiter looking for a job; the young servant looked the part in his surtout coat (a large overcoat or greatcoat), striped flannel waistcoat, buckskins and white stockings. They agreed to travel to Dover together and spent the night at the Star Inn in the same bed. At three o'clock in the morning the waiter got up, saying he needed to go into the yard, and did not return. When Thompson got up to continue his journey he discovered his money was gone, and instantly suspected the waiter. He set off on horseback in hot pursuit.

Thompson caught up with the thief, who returned some of his money, but not all. Thompson said he would ask a constable to search his pockets. To his astonishment, the thief asked if a woman could search him instead – because 'he' was a young woman!

The 'waiter', 18-year-old Mary Davis, was tried for theft at Canterbury that July. Her mannish attire caused a stir in court. She wore a: 'purple coat, green shag waistcoat, buckskin breeches, and round hat, all entirely new, and her hair powdered and curled' (*Gentleman's Magazine*, July 1784). Mary was acquitted because Thompson did not appear in court against her, perhaps embarrassed by his failure to see through her disguise.

CHAPTER 5

Shopping, 'Lounging' and Leisure

*'The pleasantness of an employment does not always
evince its propriety.'*
(Jane Austen, *Sense and Sensibility*, 1811)

London is the fashion capital: here you can go shopping, visit the theatre and hear all the latest scandal. You'll be bowled over by the brightly lit magnificence of the shops, which seem to go on for miles.

The shops open at about eight o'clock, but fashionable folk never appear before midday. Christian Goede described the scene in *The Stranger in England* (London, 1807): 'Ladies form parties to go shopping, and the gentlemen, accompanied by single grooms, go for a morning's ride... the squares fill with ladies in their morning dress, presenting lovely groupes [*sic*]... while the ladies are thus engaged, the gentlemen pass on horseback up and down the street, to see and be seen.'

At about two in the afternoon you'll see Piccadilly's long street crowded with splendid equipages and footmen, and smart gentlemen on horseback hurrying towards Hyde Park. The very 'best' society like the Prince Regent and his friends drive their carriages there. People of rank and fashion promenade, ride, or drive their carriages in Kensington Gardens, too; St James's Park has fallen from favour. The crowds head home again around three o'clock.

Fashionable young ladies head first to a mercer's or linen-draper's store. When Fanny Burney's eponymous heroine Evelina goes hunting for 'silks, caps, and gauzes', she finds the assistants keen to serve her: 'The shops are really very entertaining, especially the mercers; there seem to be six or seven men belonging to each shop; and every one took care by bowing and smirking, to be noticed.'

When Jane Austen stayed with her brother Henry and his wife Eliza in Sloane Street in 1811, she wrote to Cassandra (18 April): 'I am sorry to tell you that I am getting very extravagant and spending all my money, and, what is worse for *you,* I have been spending yours too; for in a linen-draper's shop to which I went for checked muslin, and for which I was obliged to give seven shillings a yard, I was tempted by a pretty-coloured muslin, and bought ten yards of it on the chance of your liking it… it is only 3s 6d per yard.' Austen did not walk by herself to the shops; her sister-in-law's French maidservant, Manon, accompanied her on this trip.

When you are in town, your family and friends at home will saddle you with a long shopping list. During another London visit, Jane complained to Cassandra (26 November 1815): 'We were very busy all yesterday; from half-past 11 till 4 in the streets, working almost entirely for other people, driving from place to place… and encountering the miseries of Grafton House [*a linen-draper*] to get a purple frock for Eleanor Bridges.'

The 'Hermit in London', Felix M'Donogh, sketched the characters he saw in a linen-draper's shop on the Strand:

> The superb dame who is there from idleness, and buys everything; the… fashionable [*lady*] who shops from vacancy of mind and habit, and who turns over everything without the least intention of purchasing; the boarding-school miss who looks wistfully at a rich aunt, but cannot soften her heart into a purchase of a lace veil or a French shawl; the arch Cyprian [*lady of ill repute*] who eyes an embroidered gown and the linen-draper, or some chance male customer in the shop, with equal fondness; and lastly, the adroit shoplifter.

If you get tired while shopping, stop at a pastry-cook's for a tart, or a confectioner's for an ice-cream; confectioners serve soup, too.

Gunter's at Berkeley Square in the West End of London is famous for its ices, jellies and cakes, and Mr Gunter's fairy-tale creations can't be surpassed if you're throwing a dinner party.

Because tradesmen give long periods of credit, it's tempting to spend more than you can afford. Young ladies should remember that a reputation for extravagance makes it difficult to attract a husband. A writer in the *Lady's Magazine* (December 1780) advised: 'Learn the real value of everything you buy... never indulge an extravagant fancy, by purchasing [a] variety of useless toys and trinkets... by producing every day some new trumpery, you gain the character of an expensive woman.'

Toy shops sell ornaments such as brooches, trinkets, purses, pocketbooks, knick-knacks, snuff-boxes and so on. In Fanny Burney's *Camilla*, the heroine and her friend go shopping in fashionable Tunbridge Wells: 'The two young ladies loitered at the window of a toy shop, struck with just admiration of the beauty and the ingenuity of the Tunbridge ware it presented to their view.'

While in town you can choose all kinds of furnishings for your home: cut glass or alabaster lamps, mirrors, turnspits, crates of china, letter seals, silver plate, even stuffed birds and animals (including rare species) in glass cases.

Make sure that you pay for all your purchases before leaving the shop. In August 1799 Jane Austen's aunt Mrs Leigh Perrot was accused of stealing some lace from the shop of Elizabeth Gregory, a Bath milliner and haberdasher. Mrs Leigh Perrot was imprisoned in Ilchester jail for several months while awaiting trial. The following March, the jury found her 'Not Guilty' (*The Trial of Jane Leigh Perrot*, 1800).

BUYING A GOWN
You'll often hear your female friends mention 'buying a gown', (i.e. buying material). Jane Austen wrote to Cassandra (25 December 1798): 'I cannot determine what to do about my new gown – I wish such things were to be bought ready-made.' In another letter (24 May 1813), Jane told Cassandra that she 'got my mother's gown – seven yards at 6s 6d' from Layton and Shear's, Bedford House, London.

Some women make their own dresses at home, perhaps helped by a maidservant. Harriet Martineau (1802–1876), daughter of a Norwich manufacturer, remembered that she made 'all my clothes, except stays and shoes, as I grew up. I platted [*plaited*] bonnets… knitted stockings as I read aloud, covered silk shoes for dances, and made all my garments.' More usually, women employ a dressmaker or mantua-maker; in June 1783 Dolly Clayton of Lostock Hall, Lancashire paid £3 for her mantua-maker's services. The mantua-maker (who may be male or female) will take your measurements, then cut out pieces of paper or cloth to create a pattern. If cloth pattern pieces are used, they will later form the lining.

In the countryside, shoppers in villages like the fictional Highbury in Austen's *Emma* have fewer shops to choose from: 'Ford's was the principal woollen-draper, linen-draper and haberdasher's shop united: the shop first in size and fashion in the place.' As local shops may have only a limited range, you'll be on the lookout for one of the travelling chapmen selling fabric, lace, ribbons, and buttons. On 11 April 1801, Parson Woodforde recorded in his diary that his niece Nancy 'bought a new Gown of Mrs Batchelor of Reepham who travels about with a Cart.'

Keeping up with the latest fashions is not easy on a limited budget. When Jane Austen's mother was first married, she could not afford a new gown for two years. Her scarlet riding habit, which she wore for morning dress, was eventually made into a cloth suit for Jane's brother Francis. To save money, alter your old gowns to bring them up to date, or dye them for a fresh look. Austen grumbled in a letter to Cassandra (2 March 1814): 'My poor old muslin has never been dyed yet. It has been promised to be done several times. What wicked people dyers are. They begin with dipping their souls in scarlet sin.'

'LOUNGERS'
Bond Street in London is famed for its luxury goods and Goede claimed that its 'toy-shops... jewellers, confectioners, and fruiterers surpass all others in magnificence.' The street becomes so full of carriages that they can hardly move along, and the pavements are

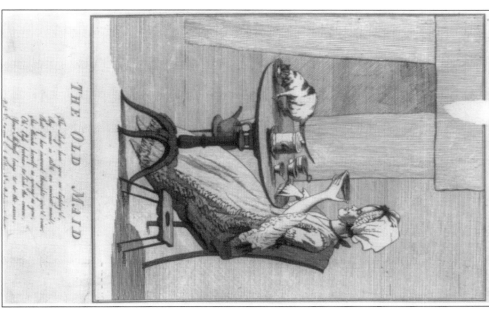

THE OLD MAID

(Left) Old maid, 1777. The fate of women unable to find their own Mr Darcy or Edward Ferrars. (Library of Congress, LC-DIG-ppmsca-19464).

The PLEASURES of the MARRIED STATE.

(Right) 'Pleasures of the married state', c.1780. Austen's heroines aspired to a happy home like this one. (Library of Congress, LC-USZ62-59621).

Natural accidents in quadrille dancing, 1817. (Library of Congress, LC-USZ62-20387).

High life: Tom and Jerry 'sporting a toe' among the Corinthians at Almack's. Engraving by George and Robert Cruikshank, *Life in London*, (John Camden Hotten, Piccadilly, 1869).

(*Above*) Tom and Jerry at Vauxhall Gardens (mentioned by Austen in her juvenilia).

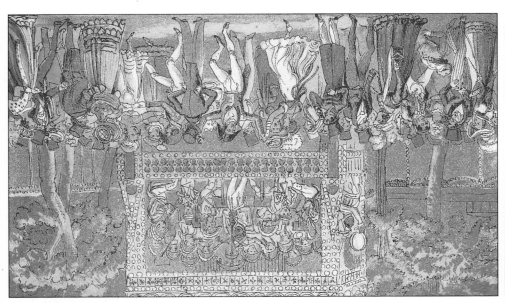

(*Below*) Tom and Jerry at Rotten Row, Hyde Park, where people of fashion showed off their finery. Both illustrations are from George and Robert Cruikshank, *Life in London*, (John Camden Hotten, Piccadilly, 1869)

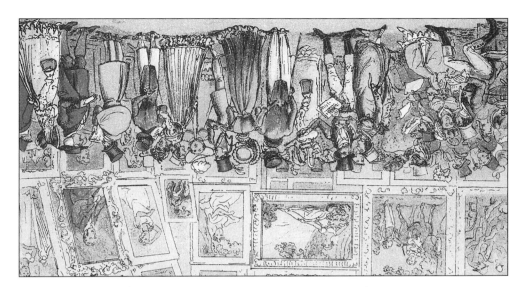

(Above) 'School for boxing', 1788. Boxing was a hugely popular sport. (Library of Congress, LC-USZ62-132988).

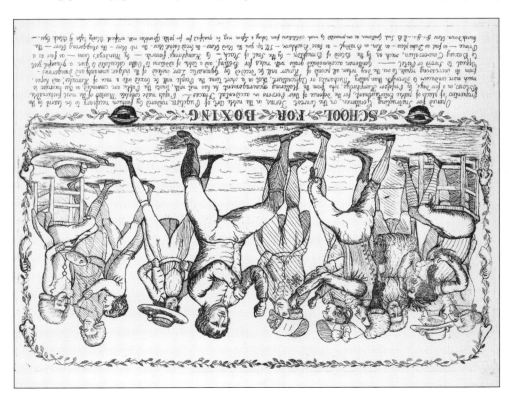

(Below) Tom and Jerry pay a shilling to see the exhibition at the Royal Academy. Jane Austen went to picture exhibitions at Spring Gardens and Pall Mall in 1813. Illustration from George and Robert Cruikshank, Life in London, (John Camden Hotten, Piccadilly, 1869).

(*Below*) 'Monstrosities of 1818', by George Cruikshank. (Library of Congress, LC-DIG-ppmsca-07806).

(*Above*) Regency Dandies. From left to right: Marquis of Londonderry, 'Kangaroo' Cooke, Captain Gronow, Lord Allen, and Count D'Orsay. Illustration from Captain Gronow's *Recollections and Anecdotes*, (Smith, Elder & Co, 1864).

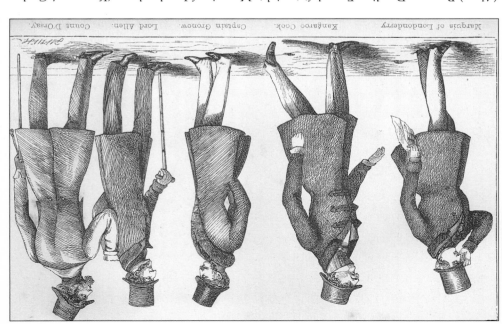

Marquis of Londonderry · Kangaroo Cook · Captain Gronow · Lord Allen · Count D'Orsay

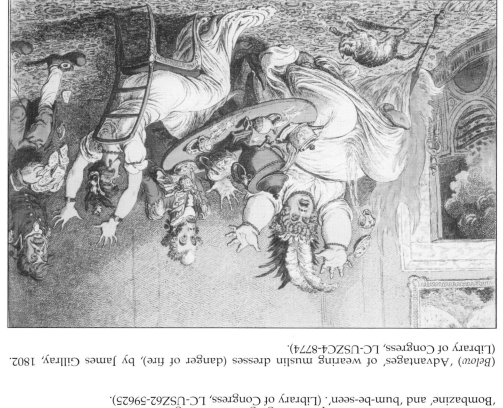

(*Above*) Muslin frocks were quite clinging. Contrasting fashions of 1740 and 1807: 'Bombazine' and 'bum-be-seen'. (Library of Congress, LC-USZ62-59625).

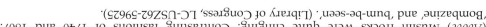

(*Below*) 'Advantages' of wearing muslin dresses (danger of fire), by James Gillray, 1802. (Library of Congress, LC-USZC4-8774).

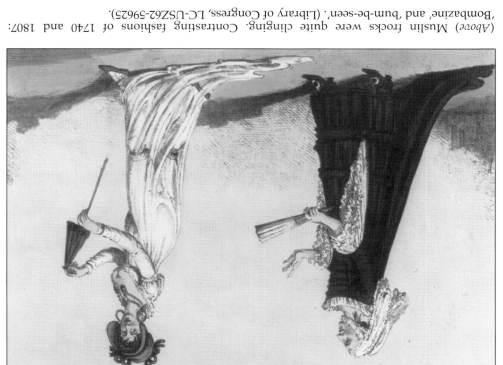

(*Left*) This fashion plate for August 1798 shows a lady wearing a 'Turban Head dress' (*figure on right*), and a chair and stool of the period.

(*Right*) Fashions for November 1798: 'Fashionable Military dress at the Presentation of Colours'. Lizzy Bennet's mother and sister Lydia were partial to gentlemen in red coats. (Both images are from the *Lady's Monthly Museum* Vol. 1, Verner & Hood, 1798).

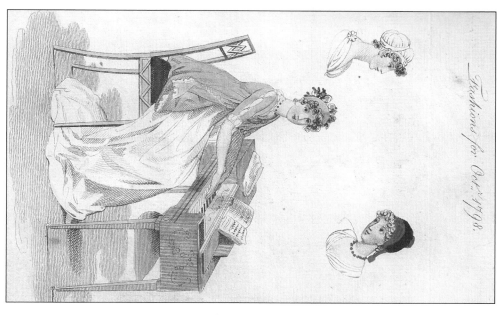

Fashions for Oct.ʳ 1798.

(Left) Fashions for October 1798. Austen played on the pianoforte every day when at home.

(Right) Fashions for October 1798. Large figure: 'Moorish habit, with ruff of muslin, edged with lace; black straw hat, with rose of coclico [sic - red], tied under the chin with ribbon of the same colour'. Note the parasol to keep the lady's complexion fair. (Both images are from the Lady's Monthly Museum Vol. 1, Verner & Hood, 1798).

Fashions for Oct.ʳ 1798.

'Lodgings to let': a young lady fends off an admirer. (Library of Congress, LC-USZC2-3806).

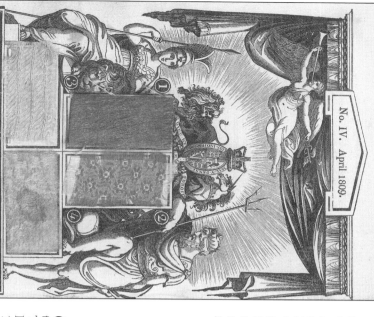

No. IV. April 1809.

The Repository

Of Arts, Literature, Commerce, Manufactures, Fashions, and Politics.

Manufacturers, Factors, and Wholesale Dealers in Fancy Goods, that come within the scope of this Plan, are requested to send Patterns of such new Articles as they come out, and if the requisites of Novelty, Fashion, and Elegance are united, the quantity necessary for this Magazine will be ordered.

R. Ackermann, 101, Strand, London.

(*Left*) Allegorical woodcut from April 1809 issue of Ackermann's *Repository of Arts*, with samples of scarlet and gold furniture calico, a striped 'Scotia silk', and a spotted muslin.

(*Right*) 'Work for the plumber', by Thomas Rowlandson, 1810. Only a lucky few had piped water indoors. (Library of Congress, LC-USZ62-22413).

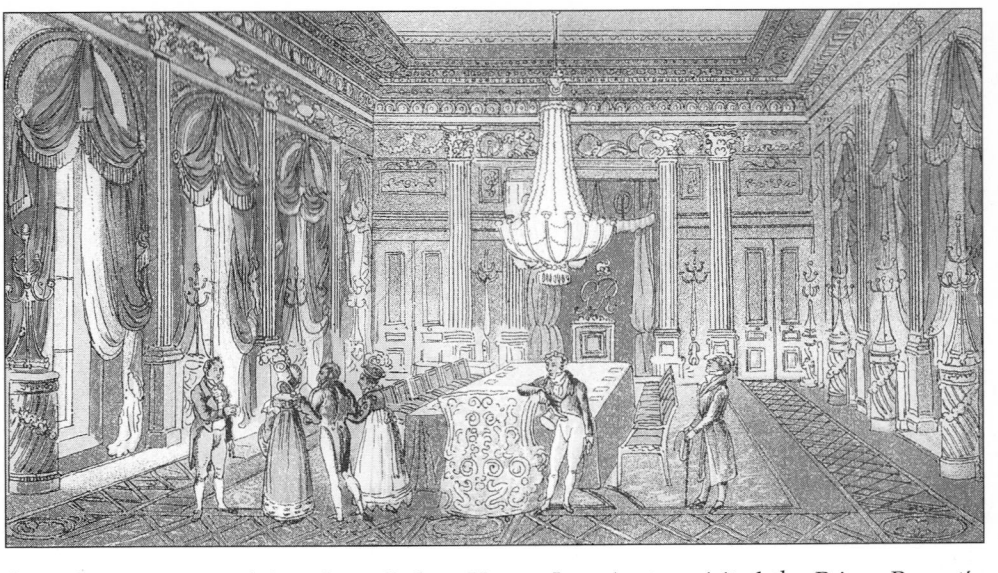

(*Above*) Tom, Jerry and friends at Carlton House. Jane Austen visited the Prince Regent's London residence in November 1815. (Image from George and Robert Cruikshank, *Life in London*, John Camden Hotten, Piccadilly, 1869).

(*Below*) 'A High Wind in the Park', by J. Baker (1819). (Library of Congress, LC-DIG-ppmsca-07807).

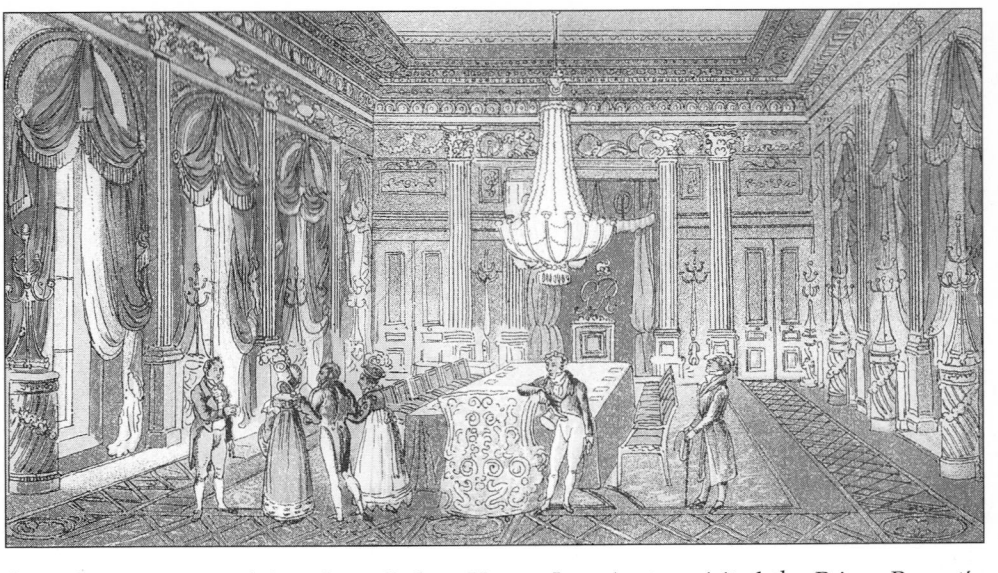

A HIGH WIND in the Park!

(*Above*) Coaching Scene, 1790s. Some gentlemen bandy words with street sellers. Illustration by John Jones (1745-1797).

(*Below*) Dandies dressing, 1818. Note the corsets and high starched neck-cloths. Cartoon by I. R. Cruickshank. (Library of Congress, LC-USZC4-3649).

(*Above*) Chawton Church. Jane Austen's mother and sister Cassandra are buried here (*Harper's New Monthly Magazine*, Vol. XLI, 1870).

(*Below*) 'It's the Comet; and you must be as quick as lightning'. Illustration by Henry T. Alken, *The Chace, The Turf and The Road* (John Murray, second edition, 1843).

(*Above*) Jane Austen (1775-1817), novelist. She only enjoyed modest success during her lifetime, but her six novels, particularly *Pride and Prejudice* (1813) are immensely popular with modern readers, and have been adapted for film and television many times.

(*Below*) Steventon Parsonage, Austen's childhood home (Both images are from *Harper's New Monthly Magazine*, Vol. XLI, 1870).

Pump Room, Bath, 1804. Engraving by John Hill from an aquatint by J. C. Nattes (Library of Congress, LC-USZ62-134778)

packed solid with elegant shoppers. This fashionable district is the natural habitat of that well known species the 'Bond Street lounger'. These coxcombs spend their days in complete idleness but they are mostly harmless.

A typical day for a lounger begins when he rises at midday. He reads the papers over breakfast before donning his riding coat. After inspecting his 'cattle' (horses) in their stable and chatting to his coachman, he'll order his curricle and dash through the streets to call at the coach and harness makers to see the latest equine accoutrements. Next the 'lounger' fritters away some time with a chatty but expensive Cyprian like Harriette Wilson before going on to Tattersall's, near Hyde Park Corner, to meet all his friends and discuss the latest horses for sale.

Tattersall's Repository is the centre of the sporting world: swarming with 'swells' (gentlemen), bucks, fox-hunting parsons, military gentlemen, jockeys and noblemen. This famous horse mart was founded in about 1773 by Richard Tattersall, according to the *Microcosm of London* (1810). Tattersall made his fortune with his celebrated racehorse 'Highflyer'.

An incredible number of carriages, horses, hounds, harnesses, etc. are auctioned here every Monday and Thursday in the winter; Mondays only in the summer. A saddle horse costs over 40 guineas; a pair of good coach horses over 150 guineas. Gentlemen addicted to 'the turf' (racing) also settle their bets here from races all over the country, in a special room: they pay a guinea per year for the privilege. Tattersall's has an elegant dining room embellished with sculptures and pictures of noted racehorses.

After Tattersall's our lounger may visit an exhibition of watercolours at Bond Street or peruse the latest caricatures in a print seller's like Ackermann's, before pausing for spruce beer and sandwiches at a hotel. Then he'll dress for dinner at home before sallying forth in his chariot to a family dinner or dinner party at a hotel. At ten o'clock he goes to the opera, where he flits from box to box, quizzing his friends. When the show has ended he makes an assignation with an opera dancer. Our hero ends his evening at a gaming 'hell' (club) before flopping into bed at about four o'clock, ready to begin another day of dissipation tomorrow.

PICKPOCKETS AND BEGGARS

Be wary of pickpockets when going shopping. They often strike when you stop to look in a shop window, or watch a street fight. Gentlemen should ask their tailor to include some inside pockets when having a new coat made up, to make it harder for thieves to steal their watch and valuables. A breast pocket is useful for carrying important papers or a pocket book. It is far safer to carry coins loose in your breeches pockets than a coin purse. A surtout coat is another good safeguard.

Because footpads and robbers may lurk in the shadows, London streets have been lit by globular lamps with oil burners since the early eighteenth century. The lamps are replaced each autumn ready for winter.

The *British Mercury* (3 November 1788) reported the 'pleasing... spectacle' of 'changing the lamps' in Marylebone:

> a hundred and twenty journeymen lamplighters, dressed in white jackets, blue aprons, etc., walked two by two, with a lamp under each arm, preceded by others bearing ladders, a foreman, etc. A cart drawn by six horses attended, for the reception of the old lamps, in which were two violins, a bassoon, etc. The heads of the horses were decorated with ribbands [*sic*], and the day concluded with the greatest... conviviality; a supper... being given by the master.

Recently, gas lighting has made it even safer to walk in the streets at night: in 1807 Pall Mall in London became the first city street to be illuminated by coal gas. Other towns and cities have followed suit: the Chester Gas Light Company was formed in 1817.

You'll often be importuned by beggars when shopping, according to John Trusler's *London Adviser and Guide* (1790), which warns you not 'to be imposed upon' as beggars may 'affect distress to excite your humanity.'

Not all beggars fake their ailments, however. Owing to the long war you'll see maimed and crippled soldiers and sailors in the city streets. In *A Morning's Walk from London to Kew*, (London, 1817) Sir Richard Phillips is distressed to see 'young men of two or three and twenty, some of whom had lost both their arms, and others both their legs!' near Chelsea Hospital, a publicly funded charity for wounded soldiers.

BOOKS AND PRINTS

London is the centre of England's publishing industry, with over 800 books and pamphlets published annually. Lackington, Allen & Co's famous 'Temple of the Muses' on Finsbury Square has over 200,000 books for sale. Booksellers' shops, like circulating libraries, are social venues. According to *A View of London* (1804), in the West End, booksellers such as Debrett's, Stockdale's and Hatchard's have all the latest newspapers and magazines and are 'frequented as lounging-places, about the middle of the day, by fashionable people.'

Fanny Burney described a Tunbridge Wells bookshop in *Camilla*: 'Mr Dennel took up the *Daily Advertiser*; his daughter stationed herself at the door to see the walkers upon the Pantiles; Sir Theophilus Jarard, under colour [*cover*] of looking at a particular pamphlet, was indulging in a nap in a corner... and Sir Sedley Clarendel, lounging upon a chair in the middle of the shop, sat eating *bon bons*.'

Author Mary Russell Mitford treated herself to several volumes from a Reading bookseller before beginning a long coach journey to Northumberland in 1806 with her father. She bought: 'a Cobbett [*probably the* Political Register, *a newspaper*]... a Cary's *Itinerary*, Peter Pindar, and a few plays.' Many young ladies love reading the latest Gothic romance such as Mrs Radcliffe's *Mysteries of Udolpho*, or moralistic tales like Fanny Burney's *Cecilia* and Maria Edgeworth's *Belinda*, 'in which the greatest powers of the mind are displayed,' as Jane Austen says in *Northanger Abbey*.

But some people think that novels are trashy and have an immoral tendency, as pompous Mr Collins in *Pride and Prejudice* makes clear when Mr Bennet asks him to read aloud to the ladies: 'On beholding it (for everything announced it to be from a circulating library), he started back, and begging pardon, protested that he never read novels.' It's common for families like the Bennets to subscribe to a circulating library because new books are so expensive (a three volume set of *Sense and Sensibility* cost 15s when first published in 1811). Circulating libraries also sell trinkets, and Lydia Bennet saw 'such beautiful ornaments as made her quite wild' in the Brighton library.

Those who can afford it amass their own library at home and George Austen had over 500 volumes at Steventon Rectory. In *Pride and Prejudice*, Mr Darcy 'cannot comprehend the neglect of a family library in such days as these.'

Nevertheless, the Austens were keen readers and subscribed to a circulating library as well. On 18 December 1798, Jane Austen wrote to Cassandra from Steventon:

> I have received a very civil note from Mrs Martin, requesting my name as a subscriber to her library... My mother finds the money... Mrs Martin tells me that her collection is not to consist only of novels, but of every kind of literature, etc. She might have spared this pretension to our family, who are great novel-readers, and not ashamed of being so; but it was necessary, I suppose, to the self-consequence of half her subscribers.

Reading is a family activity as well as entertainment for one's private hours. The Austens whiled away the long evenings with the latest publications such as Walter Scott's *Marmion* and *Waverley* and travel memoirs like James Boswell's *Journal of a Tour to the Hebrides* (1785).

Ladies can choose from several magazines including the hugely popular *Lady's Magazine* (1770 onwards), Heideloff's *Gallery of Fashion* (1794) and from 1806 *La Belle Assemblée* and *Le Beau Monde*. Magazines like these contain the latest modes with brightly coloured fashion plates. The *Lady's Monthly Museum*, first published in 1798, prints short stories, articles and biographies of famous women.

Both sexes enjoy turning the pages of the latest Ackermann publication. Rudolph Ackermann (1764–1834) opened his print-seller's shop at 101 Strand in 1797. The following year he christened his store, from which he sold artists' materials, paintings and prints: 'The Repository of Arts'. In 1810 the Repository was lit by coal gas generated by an apparatus designed by Ackermann himself. Crowds of the *beau monde*, gentry and artists flock every night to the Repository to see his latest beautiful publications. Weekly soirées for eminent artists and scientists from Britain and abroad are held there, too.

Ackermann's modish magazine *The Repository of Arts, Literature, Commerce, Manufactures, Fashions and Politics* (1809 onwards), priced at four shillings, has up-to-date news on fashion, house styles and furnishings. The magazine's success was followed by the *Microcosm of London* (1810), 'an admirable *lounging-book* for a breakfast-room', according to the *Critical Review* (July 1810). Ackermann's *Microcosm* shows all the sights of London in over 100 aquatints by Rowlandson and Pugin: Carlton House and St James's Palace, the thrills of Astley's Amphitheatre, even the forbidding walls of the Fleet and Newgate Prisons.

Conservative readers prefer the heavyweight Tory journal *Quarterly Review*, established in 1809 to combat the Whig *Edinburgh Review*. In *Mansfield Park* (1809) Fanny Price and her companions, 'lounge away the time with… chit-chat, and *Quarterly Reviews*,' after exploring Sotherton Park. The long-established *Gentleman's Magazine* prints literary reviews and notices of ecclesiastical posts and recently deceased clergy – of vital interest to would-be clergymen like *Sense and Sensibility*'s Edward Ferrars, who cannot marry Elinor Dashwood without a decent living.

The print-sellers' shops are filled with vicious caricatures penned by artists like James Gillray, Thomas Rowlandson, and the Cruikshank family. No politician, Royal personage or member of the *haut ton* is safe from their bawdy and wickedly accurate satires. The print-sellers' windows attract gently bred young ladies, as John Corry complained in his *Satirical View of London*, (London, 1815): 'It is an authenticated fact, that girls often go in parties to visit the windows of print-shops, that they may amuse themselves with the view of naked figures in the most indecent postures.'

For more cultured tastes, exhibitions of paintings are popular with both sexes. When staying in London during May 1813, Jane Austen 'had great amusement among the pictures' at the Royal Academy's exhibition at Somerset House and Sir Joshua Reynolds' paintings at Pall Mall. At another exhibition in Spring Gardens she saw a portrait just like her fictional creation Mrs Bingley (Jane Bennet in *Pride and Prejudice*): 'She is dressed in a white gown, with green ornaments... I had always supposed, that green was a favourite colour with her.' Jane hoped to find a portrait of Mrs Darcy, but was disappointed.

MEN'S CLUBS AND GAMBLING
Gambling is socially acceptable; during the 1790s titled ladies like the notorious Lady Archer ran faro tables in their own home. The deepest play takes place at the London men's clubs such as White's, Watier's and Brookes', membership of which is almost exclusively confined to the nobility, although you may be invited to join if sufficiently witty and talented.

Brookes' Club is notorious for its 'high play' – tens of thousands of pounds are bet on games like whist and hazard. It was originally set up on Pall Mall in 1764 by several noblemen including the Duke of Portland. Brookes' Club was originally known as Almack's as it was run by William Almack, who also founded the famous Assembly Rooms on King Street. Mr Goosetree took over the Pall Mall Club, then Mr Brookes, who built new premises on 60, St James's Street; the new club opened in October 1778. The Prince of Wales and Beau Brummell are both members.

White's Club at Burlington House on St James's Street is the most difficult to join, and you are unlikely to cross its threshold unless you are an aristocrat. Even then you won't be allowed to join if 'blackballed'. (When a new member is proposed, a secret ballot is held; each member chooses a white or a black ball and puts it into a bag. When the bag is emptied, a single black ball means that you are excluded). The gamesters at White's are notorious for their readiness to bet on anything – even life and death.

In June 1814 Jane Austen's brother Henry, then involved in banking, was fortunate enough to get a ticket for a grand ball at White's for over 2,000 guests, to celebrate the Treaty of Paris. Jane was flabbergasted when she heard what august company he had been keeping: 'Henry at White's! Oh, what a Henry!'

If you're bored with the monotonous fare at White's and Brookes' – the endless beef-steaks, boiled chicken with oyster sauce, and apple tart – then try one of the newest clubs, Watier's on Bolton Street, Piccadilly. According to Captain Gronow, Watier's began life as a dining club organised by the Prince Regent's chef Watier at His Royal Highness's behest in about 1807. A cook from the Royal kitchens, Labourie, was in charge of the cuisine. Not even the best Parisian cooks could beat chef Labourie's fabulous dinners.

Soon cards and dice were the order of the day at Watier's, and macao the favourite game. Beau Brummell acted as the club's president; the poet Thomas Moore, Lord Byron and Lord Alvanley (a noted wit) were members. Brummell once won £26,000 in one sitting but lost it all again a few days later.

You don't have to join a club to gamble. Bucks bet huge sums on sporting events like cock fights, dog fights, horse races, private coach races, and so on. The 'celebrated pedestrian' Captain Barclay wagered James Wedderburn-Webster 1,000 guineas that he could walk 1,000 miles in 1,000 hours at Newmarket in 1809. Thousands of people, including belted earls, turned out to witness this amazing feat. Sports writer Pierce Egan reckoned that in total bets of £100,000 (about £7.5 million in 2013) were placed on the outcome (*Sporting Anecdotes*, London, 1820). Barclay finished his race with 45 minutes to spare 'in perfect ease and great spirit.'

The upper classes regard gambling debts as debts of honour, which take precedence over money owed to tradesmen. If they don't pay their tradesmen, duns and bailiffs will descend on their home, so if someone

103

regularly gambles for high stakes it has serious consequences for their family and dependants. Mamas warn their daughters off a young man if he is a known rake or gambler. In *Pride and Prejudice*, Jane Bennet is horrified when she hears that George Wickham has 'debts of honour' and other expenses amounting to 'more than a thousand pounds... "A gamester!" she cried. "I had not an idea of it".'

The middle classes are more likely to indulge in card parties, or a flutter on the state lottery. When Mary Russell Mitford was a little girl her father, who had already exhausted his wife's fortune, won £20,000 on the lottery after Mary picked the winning number. The prize money funded a nice house, estate and carriage at Reading for the family.

Ladies and gentlemen play card games like vingt-un (pontoon), casino, speculation, whist and loo after dinner at home, or at private parties. In *Pride and Prejudice*, Elizabeth Bennet is desperate to talk to Mr Darcy after dinner at Longbourn, but he falls 'victim to her mother's rapacity for whist players' and 'they were confined for the evening at different tables.' You should only play if, like Mr Collins, you are so comfortably circumstanced that losing 'five shillings' is not an object.

Jane Austen was not so fortunate, however, and in a letter to Cassandra (7 October 1808) she grizzled: 'We found ourselves tricked into a thorough party at Mrs M.'s, a quadrille and a commerce table, and music in the other room. There were two pools at commerce, but I would not play more than one, for the stake was three shillings, and I cannot afford to lose that twice in one evening.'

ALMACK'S

The most exclusive venue of all is Almack's Assembly Rooms on King Street, St James's Square, in London. The club, founded in 1765 by William Almack, was taken over by Mr Willis in the early 1780s.

Almack's or 'Willis's Rooms' is the 'seventh heaven of the fashionable world' according to Captain Gronow. You can't attend events there without the permission of its fearsome lady patronesses: Lady Castlereagh, Lady Jersey, Lady Cowper, Lady Sefton, Mrs Drummond Burrell, Princess Esterhazy and the Countess Lieven.

These ladies receive hundreds of humble petitions for tickets or 'vouchers', and there's much heart-burning and jealousy amongst unsuccessful applicants.

Gronow said that Lady Cowper (later Lady Palmerston) was very popular; Lady Sefton was noted for her kindness. But Lady Jersey (the Prince Regent's mistress), wore the air of a 'theatrical tragedy queen'; she was 'inconceivably rude, and in her manner often ill-bred.'

There is a strict dress code: the patronesses have decreed that gentlemen must wear 'knee-breeches, white cravat, and chapeau bras'. You won't be allowed inside if incorrectly attired, even with an admission voucher. One evening, the Duke of Wellington tried to enter dressed in black trousers, but Mr Willis, the guardian of the establishment, stepped forward and said, "Your Grace cannot be admitted in trousers", so the Duke 'quietly walked away.'

People certainly do not attend Almack's for the sake of the refreshments, which are pretty mundane. Tea and orgeat (an almond-flavoured drink) are hardly strong enough to encourage love-making, as Henry Luttrell lamented in his *Letters to Julia* (John Murray, 1822):

> *...such lifeless love is made,*
> *On cakes, orgeat and lemonade,*
> *That hungry women grow unkind,*
> *And men too faint to speak their mind,*
> *Tea mars all mirth, makes evenings drag,*
> *And talk grow flat, and courtship flag,*
> *Tea, mawkish beverage, is the reason,*
> *Why fifty flirtings in a season,*
> *Swell with ten marriages, at most,*
> *The columns of the Morning Post.*

Jane Austen and her sister Cassandra did not have the right social connections to enter the hallowed portals of Almack's. However, their cousin Eliza de Feuillide did and in 1787 she attended an assembly there after attending Court in full dress. She wrote to her cousin Phila Walter: 'I... stood from two to four in the drawing-room and of course loaded with a great hoop of no inconsiderable weight, went to the Duchess of Cumberland's in the evening and from thence to Almack's, where I staid [*sic*] till five in the morning.'

MUSIC AND CULTURE

A public concert is a good opportunity to meet members of the opposite sex, as well as being an amusing spectacle. Formerly, when Austen was a young girl, visitors flocked to hear evening concerts at the magnificent rotunda in Ranelagh Gardens at Chelsea, London. Fanny Burney's Evelina thought Ranelagh 'a charming place... the brilliancy of the lights, on my first entrance, made me almost think I was in some enchanted castle or fairy palace, for all looked like magic to me.' The gardens were a favourite spot for romantic assignations.

As the years passed, the fashionable set voted Ranelagh boring and inconveniently situated, and it was gradually eclipsed by its rival, Vauxhall Gardens. In the late 1780s, Ranelagh's fortunes briefly revived, thanks to the Prince of Wales' patronage. On 7 June 1790 over 4,000 people paid 3s 6d to see a grand firework exhibition, and in June 1802 the celebrated aeronaut M. Garnerin made a balloon ascent from the gardens. But Ranelagh's glories faded and the gardens opened for the last time on 8 July 1803.

Vauxhall Gardens, about a mile-and-a-half from the centre of London, are still immensely popular. A visitor in 1810 pays 3s 6d for admission; the gardens open on Monday, Wednesday and Friday, and thousands of people throng its groves in the evenings. As you explore Vauxhall's long avenues of trees, you'll be astounded by the illuminations: over 30,000 lights blaze out, some behind painted transparencies, and the walks and arbours are splendidly decorated. The orchestra building is in the form of a Grecian temple and lit by 4,000 lamps; the magnificent rotunda is a finely painted pavilion 70ft in diameter, with a long supper room alongside.

The main concert begins at eight o'clock, followed by a waterworks display: a curtain rises to show a watermill, cascade and bridge, with coaches and waggons passing over it. After more music, a bell announces the start of the firework display. You'll end your evening with a cold collation in one of the alcoves or 'boxes'. Vauxhall's ham slices are famously meagre: Benjamin Silliman wrote: 'the ham was shaved so thin, that it served rather to excite than to allay the appetite.'

You may be invited to a musical concert given by friends or family. When Jane Austen stayed with her brother Henry and his wife Eliza in April 1811, they threw a concert at Sloane Street attended by over 60 people. They hired glee singers, a harpist and pianoforte player; Jane said that 'the music was extremely good.'

Your stay in London won't be complete without going to a show like the amazing equestrian exploits at Astley's Amphitheatre at Westminster Bridge, which has the largest stage in England. The horses perform wonderful feats such as country dances. Jane Austen went to Astley's in 1796 and in her novel *Emma*, Robert Martin proposed to Emma's friend Harriet Smith the day after being 'extremely amused' by a trip to Astley's.

Theatregoing is *de rigeur* and actors like Edmund Kean and the tragedienne Sarah Siddons bring audiences flocking in. Kean's acting is so authentic and overpowering that women (including his fellow actresses) faint during his performances. Jane Austen often visited Covent Garden and other theatres; she saw *The Hypocrite* at the Lyceum (which was lit by gas) in April 1811. Jane was very disappointed when she missed seeing Sarah Siddons that year. But she had better luck with Kean, who she saw three years later: 'I cannot imagine better acting,' Jane wrote to Cassandra.

Although all classes of society visit the theatre, only members of the nobility can afford a regular box at the Opera House, which costs a hefty 200 guineas annually, according to John Corry. (The Opera House, near the bottom of the Haymarket, was built 1704–5 and was formerly the Queen's Theatre). If you require refreshments after going to a play or a concert, you can meet friends for fruit or ices at Grange's in Piccadilly, which stays open after the Opera House has closed.

Other famous theatres (circa 1802) include Covent Garden Theatre (Bow Street), Drury Lane (Brydges Street), the Theatre Royal (on the Haymarket), and Sadler's Wells. Until recently Sadler's Wells was famous for its tumbling and rope-dancing acts. Margaret Pedder of

Lancashire visited Sadler's Wells on 27 May during her London jaunt in 1789: 'was much pleased with the performance, one Richard was very cleaver [*sic*] on the rope dancing and the scenery is very good.'

Nowadays the entertainment at Sadler's Wells is more sophisticated, according to the *Gentleman's Magazine* (December 1813). Performances begin with a 'light comic dance, a serious ballet, a short pantomime, occasionally rope-dancing, and a grand historical spectacle.' In April 1804 one of the most stunning finales was the *Siege of Gibraltar*, in which the stage flooring moved to reveal 'floating boats, ships and sea-monsters' on water from the nearby New River.

Gentlemen can hardly fail to notice the many elegantly and skimpily dressed women in the theatre lobbies, and the streets nearby; they are common street-walkers after the contents of your pocket book. The darker groves of Vauxhall Gardens are also a hunting ground for prostitutes. One evening Christian Goede spotted: 'A number of bucks of the first class' getting ready for a night out by visiting an 'apothecary's shop' in a side street, where they 'intoxicated themselves with fumes of oxygen, which is... sold as a powerful aphrodisiac at half a guinea a dose.'

SUNDAYS

On a fine Sunday in London, you can hardly climb into your barouche without being hustled by men-milliners, linen-drapers and other 'cits'. Fashionable Hyde Park is invaded by tens of thousands of the middling sort and the *beau monde* give them a wide berth. The roads out of London are filled with carriages as the 'gay and the wealthy' spend 'their Sabbaths in the country... frequenting the village-churches,' according to traveller Christian Goede.

Card playing is frowned on, and the London theatres are closed. You can't go clothes shopping either. American Benjamin Silliman noticed that: 'the shops are generally shut, but those of the pastry-cooks are kept open, and although the markets are closed, fruits, walking-sticks and Sunday newspapers are hawked round the streets.'

Most respectable folk like you attend church on Sundays, unless they are unwell or the weather is especially inclement. Important local families have their own pew, like the Tilneys in *Northanger Abbey*. The more active clergymen give twice-daily Sunday services, like the ones held at St Nicholas's Church in Chawton, which Jane Austen attended. But many small churches hold just a morning or evening service.

If you find a clergyman's sermons particularly inspiring, you may write them down in your pocket book or stitch a choice phrase into a sampler. *Emma*'s Miss Nash, a fan of Mr Elton, 'put down all the texts he has ever preached from since he came to Highbury.'

In London, fashionable upper and middle class folk attend divine service at one of the charitable institutions like the Foundling Hospital for the care and education of abandoned infants. Silliman 'heard an excellent sermon from Mr Hewlet' there and enjoyed 'the singing of the Foundlings' which was 'soft, melodious and natural.' The chapel at the Magdalen House for reclaiming penitent female prostitutes is another popular venue. Christian Goede explained that it was:

> Much frequented on Sundays, when collections are made for the benefit of the charity. The girls sit in the choir of the chapel behind green hangings, which conceal them from the view of the public. Their singing is much celebrated, and the solemnity of the service so moving, that I have known several Londoners who preferred it to all others in the metropolis.

The 'enthusiasm' of the Evangelical movement is becoming increasingly fashionable, although the texts preached by some firebrand preachers are not to everyone's taste. During her stay in London, young Margaret Pedder heard the famous Methodist, Rowland Hill (1744–1833), who often preached at Surrey Chapel at Blackfriars Road, London. Hill founded the chapel in 1783.

On 24 May 1789 Margaret was: 'at the Foundling Hospital in the Morning... heard a good sermon from the Clergyman there Dr Pinnock dined at two o'Clock intend [*intended*] going to the Magdalene in the Evening but finding we was [*sic*] so late we stopt [*sic*] at Rowland Hill's Chapple [*sic*]… astonishing the crowd that was there to hear his foolish doctrine we did not stop long he was very vehement.' Margaret later married Dr David Campbell of Lancaster.

THE WILD ONES

The Tower of London is open to visitors on Sundays, even though it's still used as a state prison. You can explore the Royal armouries and see the sparkling magnificence of the crown jewels and Royal regalia. According to *A View of London* (1803), for 1s 6d you can see the 'the imperial crown with which kings of England are crowned; the golden globe, and the golden sceptre,' worn by the king at his coronation. The Mint is housed in the Tower but visitors are banned for security reasons, even though the process of coining is said to be extremely interesting.

The Tower is also renowned for His Majesty's collection of wild beasts, situated in a yard by the west entrance. For another shilling you can marvel at 'the most remarkable wild beasts... a young lion, four lionesses, five tygers [*sic*], three leopards, one panther; three bears, two racoons [*sic*], a spotted hyena, and a wolf.'

Jane Austen's sister Cassandra is said to have visited another collection, Pidcock's famous menagerie in Exeter Change on the Strand, London in 1801. Benjamin Silliman saw lions, tigers, kangaroos, monkeys and baboons there during his London stay. Silliman was most impressed by the elephant, which entertained him with tricks such as picking up Benjamin's walking cane with his trunk, and extricating money from his waistcoat pocket.

In 1810 Londoners were startled to see a leopard strolling down the Haymarket with a regal air. Mr Wombwell, owner of another noted zoo at Piccadilly, had put the leopard into a caravan to take it to Bartholomew Fair. But the horse pulling the caravan took fright, bolted into the Haymarket, and the vehicle was overturned. The leopard took this opportunity to escape, pausing only to bite his keeper. It was later recaptured.

In this enlightened age, the fashionable set visit institutions for the cure of 'lunatics', where human beings are kept in conditions little better than a zoo. For example, if you obtain a ticket of admission from

110

one of the governors, you can gawp at the inmates of Bethlem Royal Hospital at Moorfields, London. At 'Bedlam', as it is colloquially known, men and women spend their days practically naked (except for a blanket gown), chained and fettered, and lying on straw. In 1803 Bethlem is open to visitors on Mondays, Wednesdays and Fridays.

The Moorfields site was shut down owing to its bad state of repair, so Benjamin Silliman could not see it when he visited London in 1805. Instead he explored a similar institution, St Luke's Hospital, near Finsbury Square. Although this building was 'neat, clean' and 'airy', Silliman thought it 'one of the most pitiable and affecting sights I have ever beheld. Some [*patients*] were merry and full of glee, and declared that they were perfectly well... some were fixed in sullen death-like melancholy... others were actuated by furious madness, clanging their chains, gnashing their teeth, and screaming piteously.'

Bethlem was rebuilt at St George's Fields in 1812. Sadly the inmates did not enjoy more humane treatment until a parliamentary inquiry three years later highlighted their dreadful living conditions, and a kindlier regime was put in place. The institution was still open to the public, however, and attracted several hundred visitors annually.

A POINT OF HONOUR

You should take fencing and shooting lessons, like many other young bucks, in case you find yourself facing a determined adversary in the cold light of dawn. Gentlemen still feel compelled to defend their honour at sword or gunpoint. In *Sense and Sensibility*, Colonel Brandon challenges Willoughby to a duel after he seduces the colonel's young relative, Eliza Williams, and leaves her destitute and pregnant: both men survive the duel unwounded. Elinor Dashwood: 'sighed over the fancied necessity of this; but to a man and a soldier she presumed not to censure it.'

Duelling is not illegal *per se*, but if a duellist dies, his opponent may be charged with premeditated murder. In 1787 gentlemen frequented the fencing academy on the Haymarket run by Henry Angelo, who taught the Prince of Wales and Duke of Gloucester how to balance a blade.

111

A duel may be triggered by a seemingly trivial offence. In 1806, the poet Thomas Moore's Irish blood boiled following a scathing review of his poems by Francis Jeffrey in the *Edinburgh Review.* He challenged Jeffrey to a duel and bought pistols and ammunition in a Bond Street shop. Fortunately the duel (at Chalk Farm) was stopped by some Bow Street Runners. Moore and Jeffrey were arrested and taken before the Bow Street magistrates, and their guns examined. To Moore's dismay, it was found that his pistol was loaded but Jeffrey's was not: the ball had fallen out, probably when the duel was interrupted.

A rumour spread that both pistols were unloaded, implying that the duellists were cowards; Moore wrote to the newspapers in an attempt to clear his name. Meanwhile, Lord Byron mocked Moore's 'leadless pistol' in his poem *English Bards and Scotch Reviewers* (1809). Moore sent a challenge to Byron but his lordship had gone abroad. The two poets later became great friends.

Charles John Cary, 8th Viscount Falkland was not so lucky. In the spring of 1809 Lord Falkland was killed by his friend Mr Powell in a duel with pistols; Falkland had repeatedly called Powell by an offensive nickname while drunk.

Joseph Manton's shooting gallery on Davies Street is the best place to practise shooting a 'wafer' (target); crack shots like Lord Byron, Lord Yarmouth and Captain Gronow can often be seen there, betting on their skill. Captain Gronow served in the Peninsular Wars and at Waterloo and is a noted duellist. Manton is famous as a gun manufacturer, too, and sporting gentlemen buy fine duelling pistols and fowling pieces of his design.

Learning to box comes in handy in case you have to defend yourself in a dust-up with a coachman or costermonger. Not everyone is keen on these manly arts. One of John Beresford's *Miseries of Human Life* is permitting 'a great raw-boned fellow (to)... thresh [*thrash*] you... 3 or 4 times a week because you <u>may</u>, some time or other, have a fancy to thresh someone else.'

Champion boxer 'Gentleman' Jackson's famous academy on Bond Street is favoured by many young gentlemen like Lord Byron. In the early 1800s Louis Simond was introduced to 'professor of pugilism' Jackson: '[*he*] keeps a school for the fashionables of London. He is the finest figure of a man I ever saw; all muscle.'

Sparring matches (displays of skill) are regularly held in the Fives Court in St Martin's Street. Prize-fighting or boxing for money is illegal but thousands of the 'fancy' (boxing fans), including many noblemen, flock to see a fight or 'mill' when one is staged. Moulsey Hurst, on the banks of the river Thames, in Surrey, is a favourite spot for duels and prize fights.

SPORTS

Gentlemen love hunting, shooting and fishing. In 1813 Lord Wellington (later the Duke) was so addicted to fox hunting that he took a pack of hounds with him on the Peninsular campaign.

It's not unknown for men to break their necks when jumping horses over hedges and ditches, so *Mansfield Park's* Fanny Price feels alarmed instead of obliged to Henry Crawford when he lends her sailor brother William a horse. She was 'by no means convinced... that he was at all equal to the management of a high-fed hunter in an English fox-chase. When it was proved, however, to have done William no harm, she could allow it to be a kindness.'

You can't just take out a gun and shoot hares and partridges wherever you like. The killing of game by using dogs or a gun is restricted by law to members of the landed gentry, providing they own estates worth at least £100 p.a., or lease land worth at least £150 p.a. Although the countryside is plentifully stocked with fish and game, a poor man who helps himself to a hare or salmon to feed his family faces jail or transportation.

Gentlemen qualified to shoot game can grant permission (a 'deputation') to one of their tenants. When *Persuasion's* feckless Sir Walter Elliot is pondering whether to allow the Crofts to rent Kellynch Hall, Admiral Croft says he 'would be glad of the deputation, certainly.'

Some ladies go fox hunting, but in general men indulge in blood sports. Both sexes enjoy going to the races, however. Jane Austen's brother Henry attended Canterbury races in August 1814. In *Northanger Abbey*, Catherine Morland is bored silly by John Thorpe's tales of 'horses which he had bought for a trifle and sold for incredible sums; of racing matches, in which his judgement had infallibly told the winner', and 'shooting parties' in which he had 'killed more birds' than any of his companions.

KEEPING IN TOUCH

The postman's knock is your signal that news from absent friends and relatives has arrived. In 'The Letter-Bell' (*The Mirror*, 1831), William Hazlitt wrote: 'The dustman's-bell, with its heavy, monotonous noise, and the brisk, lively tinkle of the muffin-bell, have something in them, but not much. The postman's double-knock at the door the next morning... often goes to the heart!'

Ladies write to their family and friends to exchange family news, and about business matters such as enquiring about a servant's references. But *Pride and Prejudice*'s new bride Lydia Bennet claims that: 'Married women have never much time for writing. My sisters may write to *me*. They will have nothing else to do.'

Gentlemen in town for the season rely on their land agent and other servants for the day-to-day running of their estates, so they keep in contact by letter. Miss Bingley comments saucily to Mr Darcy: 'How many letters you must have occasion to write in the course of a year! Letters of business, too! How odious I should think them!'

Because the recipients of your letters pay the postage, fill each sheet with as much news as possible, writing 'across' the page at right angles if necessary to minimise the cost. It can take two or three days to complete a letter. In *Persuasion* (1818), Mary Musgrove wrote to Anne Elliot after her sister-in-law Louisa's nasty accident at Lyme Regis: 'I kept my letter open, that I might send you word how Louisa bore her journey.'

Letters are written with a goose quill and ink. The finished letter is folded into a neat package, then sealed with a bit of sealing wax or glued with a 'wafer' or blob of adhesive. Members of parliament enjoy free postage – a 'frank' – so you can save your correspondents much expense if a friendly MP 'franks' your letters. London residents use the pre-paid penny post for letters sent within a ten-mile radius of the city. Send these letters from one of the special 'penny-post' offices (not the General Post Office); deliveries are four times daily. In 1801 the penny-post charge was increased to two pence, and beyond that distance it cost three pence for letters delivered beyond the boundaries of London, Southwark and Westminster ('off the stones').

Letters for delivery outside the capital should be taken by your servant to the General Post Office on Lombard Street. Or you can give a letter to one of the 'letter-carriers' dressed in scarlet and gold who hurry through each district from five until six in the evening, ringing a bell. To send banknotes by post, cut each note in half and send the two halves separately; the bank will make good any loss providing you can produce one half of the note.

Deliveries in the provinces may be twice daily, depending on the size of the town. In small country villages with no post office, mail is left at the inn and family members either go themselves or send their servants to collect it.

Friends and acquaintances leave mail at the nearest inn if passing through. Jane Austen wrote to her sister: 'My dear Cassandra, I should not have thought it necessary to write to you so soon, but for the arrival of a letter from Charles to myself. It was written last Saturday... and conveyed to Popham Lane by Captain Boyle on his way to Midgham.' (Steventon Rectory was midway between two coach roads; the nearest inns were Deane Gate and Popham Lane).

You will be expected to read aloud your letters to visitors. Their interest will depend on the writer's skill and the freshness of the news. In Austen's *Emma*, Miss Woodhouse has heard Miss Bates' letters from Jane Fairfax far too often for politeness: 'One is sick of the very name of Jane Fairfax. Every letter from her is read forty times over; her compliments to all friends go round and round again; and if she does but send her aunt the pattern of a stomacher, or knit a pair of garters for her grandmother, one hears of nothing else for a month.'

A letter can be a good way to guide a son or daughter far from home. When Frank Austen joined an East Indiaman in his teens, his father sent him a long letter full of kindly advice. Frank treasured the letter, which he kept until the day he died.

Letter-writing is an important art, and if you are lost for words, copy some choice phrases from one of the books of standard letters for every occasion. The Rev Thomas Cooke's *Universal Letter-Writer* (London, 1812) contains letters for dealing with debtors and creditors, servants, family matters, even love, courtship and marriage. For example, 'Letter LXVIII' is a marriage proposal to a young lady from a 'real admirer' who wished to: 'make it my principal study of my future life to spend my days in the company of her whom I do prefer to all others in the world.' Several more exemplary epistles are necessary while the young lady consults her guardian, until finally the couple find true happiness.

CHAPTER 6

The Perfect Partner

'Happiness in marriage is entirely a matter of chance.'
(Jane Austen, *Pride and Prejudice*, 1813)

When you venture into polite society, your manners must be perfect, and correctly adapted to your company. Even a rich bachelor such as *Pride and Prejudice*'s Mr Darcy can 'disgust' a whole ballroom if his manners are too 'proud' and 'above his company'.

The eldest daughter of a family is always addressed as 'Miss' followed by her surname, e.g. Jane, the eldest Bennet girl, is 'Miss Bennet'. The younger daughters are addressed as 'Miss' followed by their first name and surname, e.g. 'Miss Elizabeth Bennet'. It is most impolite to address a lady or gentleman by their Christian name unless you are a close relative.

In *Emma,* Miss Woodhouse is appalled by Mrs Elton's overfamiliarity – she calls Mr Knightley 'Knightley' and Jane Fairfax by her full name, instead of 'Miss Fairfax': 'Heavens! Let me not suppose that she dares go about Emma Woodhouse-ing me! But, upon my honour, there seem no limits to the licentiousness of that woman's tongue!' Frank Churchill, too, Jane's secret fiancé, is upset when he hears '"Jane"... bandied between the Eltons, with all the vulgarity of needless repetition, and all the insolence of imaginary superiority.'

LOOKING FOR MR RIGHT
A young lady is not on the marriage market until she is 'out'. If you are not yet 'out', then your opportunities for enjoying yourself will be

limited until you are old enough to dance at public balls and assemblies. *Mansfield Park*'s Mary Crawford asks Edmund Bertram if Fanny Price is 'out': 'Does she go to balls? Does she dine out everywhere, as well as at my sister's?' When Edmund replies that he does not think Fanny has ever been to a ball, Mary is satisfied: 'Oh, then the point is clear. Miss Price is *not* out.'

Young ladies usually come 'out' when they are 17 or 18 years old. Their younger sisters wait their turn until their sibling is married or engaged, which is why the forthright Lady Catherine de Bourgh is so shocked to hear that Elizabeth Bennet's sisters are 'all five out at once? Very odd! And you only the second. The younger ones out before the elder are married!'

Aristocratic young ladies cannot attend grand social occasions in London until they have been presented at court, although they may go to smaller events in the provinces. Frances Winckley (later Lady Shelley) had her first London season in 1805, when she was 18 years old; she was presented at court on Queen Charlotte's birthday.

Your first season as a belle does not have to be in London, however; the Hon. Amelia Murray came 'out' at Blandford Races. In Austen's unfinished novel *The Watsons*, Miss Emma Watson makes 'her first public appearance' at a winter assembly in a Surrey town, where a 'long list of county families' and the Osbornes, the local nobility, are expected to attend.

If your mother can't accompany you to a ball, an aunt or older lady friend will act as your chaperone to make sure you behave correctly, and keep you safe from the attentions of unsuitable young men. In *Mansfield Park* Fanny Price sits out several dances 'most unwillingly, among the chaperons at the fire, longing for the re-entrance of her elder cousin, on whom all her own hopes of a partner then depended.'

Young ladies must guard their reputation at all times; a male relative or servant should accompany you when travelling. *Emma*'s Miss Woodhouse is very concerned to hear that Jane Fairfax wants to walk home (only a 20-minute journey) alone from Donwell Abbey: 'It is too far, indeed it is, to be walking quite alone. Let my father's servant go with you. Let me order the carriage. It can be round in five minutes.'

But Jane, desperate for some time on her own, resolutely refuses. Emma does not enjoy solitary walking, 'it was not pleasant,' and her protégé Harriet Smith is useful as a walking companion.

Pride and Prejudice's Lady Catherine de Bourgh insists it would be 'highly improper' for Elizabeth Bennet and Maria Lucas to travel unaccompanied by post: 'Young women should always be properly guarded and attended, according to their situation in life.' Elizabeth reassured her ladyship that her uncle would send a servant for them.

You should be polite to, but not over-familiar with, the young men to whom you are introduced. Excessive flirting and unladylike behaviour can have dire consequences. Theresa Hatton's homily on 'Mirth: How Far to be Indulged' in the February 1805 issue of *The Lady's Monthly Museum* contains an awful warning of Adeliza's fate: 'Romping, ridiculous jokes, frequent and loud bursts of laughter, and flirting and coquetting with the men, were her only amusements, till all her lovers and danglers fell off, and left her totally unattended.' Adeliza, thwarted in love, succumbed to: 'despair and anguish... she now dwindles out the remainder of her earthly existence, unhappy, fretful, and comfortless.'

A young lady must keep pure and chaste if she wants to attract a husband. In this society 'the loss of virtue' in females is an 'irretrievable' step which leads to 'endless ruin', as Mary Bennet says in *Pride and Prejudice*. When Wickham and Lydia Bennet live together before they are married, Lydia's 'infamy' is not just a black mark on her own character – her sisters' marital prospects are marred by her disgrace. 'For who', as Lady Catherine de Bourgh points out, 'will connect themselves with such a family?'

Common prudence dictates that you choose a partner with similar values, whom you can respect and esteem. When you are invited to balls and assemblies, your parents will ensure that you mix with young men of a similar rank, for as Mrs Lanfear says in her *Letters To Young Ladies On Their Entrance Into the World*, (London, 1824): 'Unequal marriages, whether the disparity be in years, rank, or fortune, but seldom prove happy.'

In *Pride and Prejudice*, Mr Bennet is extremely worried by Mr Darcy's proposal to Elizabeth: 'I know that you could be neither happy nor respectable, unless you truly esteemed your husband; unless you looked up to him as a superior. Your lively talents would place you in the greatest danger in an unequal marriage. You could scarcely escape discredit and misery.' A rich spouse is desirable but: 'The principle of marrying for money is in itself sordid, and inimical to domestic happiness,' Mrs Lanfear explains, although she adds, 'love-matches do not always prove the happiest.'

If you meet a young man you prefer above all others, like Jane Bennet in *Pride and Prejudice*, keep your manners calm and collected, to 'guard... from the suspicions of the impertinent'. But if you are anxious for your own establishment, you may agree with Charlotte Lucas: 'In nine cases out of ten, a woman had better show *more* affection than she feels.'

If all goes well, you'll receive a proposal from an eligible young man in your first season. If no one suitable makes an offer after your first few seasons, then by your late twenties people will think you are getting too long in the tooth for the marriage market. *Persuasion*'s Elizabeth Elliot, eldest daughter of Sir Walter, is 'still quite as handsome as ever,' but at 29 years old, she feels the approach of 'the years of danger' and 'would have rejoiced to be certain of being properly solicited by baronet-blood within the next twelvemonth or two.'

Mrs Lanfear recommends that a young lady studies a man's character, intelligence and religious principles before accepting a proposal from him. A sensible girl does not throw all caution to the winds and let love conquer all. But having made her choice, she should stick to it, even if money worries mean that she cannot marry immediately. A young woman should not be so terrified of becoming an old maid that she jumps at the first offer she receives; if she is lucky enough to be financially independent, 'a state of celibacy... is far preferable to an imprudent or ill-assorted marriage.'

The author Mary Wollstonecraft (later the wife of William Godwin) disapproved of young women marrying too soon. In *Thoughts on the Education of Daughters* (J. Johnson, 1787) she commented: 'Many [*girls*] are but just returned from a boarding school, when they are placed at the head of a family, and how fit they are to manage it, I leave the judicious to judge.' Young girls did not have enough experience of the world to make an informed choice: 'Many women, I am persuaded, marry a man before they are twenty, whom they would have rejected some years after.'

LOOKING FOR MISS RIGHT

If you have plenty of money, like Mr Bingley or Mr Darcy, be on your guard against match-making mamas, such as *Pride and Prejudice*'s Mrs Bennet. She is obsessed with finding suitable husbands for her daughters: 'The business of her life was to get her daughters married; its solace was visiting and news.' Husband-hunting ladies will pursue you with great tenacity, so steer clear of those like the 'cunning' Miss Bingley.

Don't talk to a young lady in public unless you are sure she is 'out'. In *Mansfield Park*, Tom Bertram 'got into a dreadful scrape' when walking along Ramsgate pier with the Sneyd family. Tom made a formal bow and made himself agreeable to one of Mrs Sneyd's daughters, who seemed 'perfectly easy in her manners' and dressed 'with veils and parasols like other girls; but I afterwards found that I had been giving all my attention to the youngest, who was not *out*, and had most excessively offended the eldest. Miss Augusta ought not to have been noticed for the next six months; and Miss Sneyd, I believe, has never forgiven me.'

Dinner and tea parties are a good way to meet the fair sex. When you first go to town, if staying on your own for the first time, take letters of introduction from your father or family friends so that you can mix socially. When Thomas Moore stayed in London for the first time in April 1799, he wrote to his mother: 'I thank my father from my heart for his letter to Mrs McM., and will fly to her with it immediately… I need never be out of company if I chose [*sic*] it… if I had indulged in going out often… there is scarce a night that I should not be at some female gossip party, to drink tea, play a little crambo [*a rhyming game*], and eat a sandwich.'

If you are a young clergyman with good prospects like *Emma*'s Mr Elton (who has 'independent property' as well as the Highbury living), you'll be in great demand socially. Harriet Smith gushes to her friend Miss Woodhouse: '[*Mr Elton's*] company [*is*] so sought after, that every body says he need not eat a single meal by himself if he does not choose it; that he has more invitations than there are days in the week.'

Gentlemen sometimes find gatherings like these unbearably tedious, however. John Egerton, a clergyman in his late twenties, confided to his diary (30 March 1823): 'Walked with Charles to Blackheath. Dined with Mr Lucas – Dreadfully dull Evening – his daughter and niece did nothing but giggle to one another; <u>Mem: Not to go there again.</u>'

You may have to look for romance locally if your family doesn't have a house in town. The diary entries of Daniel Vawdrey (1771–1844) of Middlewich, Cheshire may be typical of many young men trying to enjoy an active social life whilst living at home under their parents' supervision. On Tuesday 20 Nov 1792, Daniel ventured into the home of a local 'chaste nymph' but was dumbfounded to find:

> her excellency Mrs Vernon [*the nymph's mother?*] and my Father. I totter'd in, sat myself down in a dark and obscure corner of the room and hid my face... until I was haul'd out to play at quadril [*sic*], at which game I profited 1s, went from there with Miss Becket home, was very gallant, sat with her up in a corner, got to close quarters, but was repuls'd, again attempted, but could not achieve my designs, therefore made an honourable retreat to my Uncle John's.

Daniel then had supper at his uncle's and had better luck with an 'amiable damsel' there, who he 'kissed rite [*sic*] heartily.' He 'staggered home rather replete with ale at 12 – Found my Father and Mother sitting up for me, was told by my Father I was drunk <u>then</u>, which to be sure I could not deny, and also that I was going into a very bad way of life.' In the morning Daniel was lectured by his father on his wicked ways and was 'vex'd at myself – deserved it fully.'

Daniel turned out well in the end: in 1804 he married Anne, daughter of land agent Benjamin Wyatt of Lime Grove. Vawdrey became a local magistrate, inherited Tushingham Hall when his father died, and was also a respected agriculturalist.

One gentleman had such exacting standards for his future wife that he tried to 'manufacture' one to suit. The wealthy Thomas Day (1748–89) was a member of the famous Lunar Society of Birmingham. A slave trade abolitionist and a disciple of Rousseau, Day was greatly impressed by Rousseau's ideas on education. In his famous novel *Émile* (1762), Rousseau tries to show that boys should be brought up as close to nature as possible, learning by experience. Girls do not need to be educated rationally: their role in life is to please men.

Accordingly, Thomas abstracted two girls from orphanages and named them Sabrina and Lucretia. He took them to France to educate them according to Rousseau's precepts so that one girl could become the perfect wife (one was a spare). He taught them to read and write, and tried to instil in them a hatred of fripperies like fashion, fine titles and luxuries. While the girls were growing up, Day became enamoured of several genteel women, none of whom were prepared to conform to his ideas of wifely perfection. Meanwhile, Lucretia did not cope well with Day's training programme and he was forced to abandon the experiment. He gave her some money and she later married a shopkeeper.

However, Thomas became more and more attached to Sabrina, and their friends expected them to marry. According to Richard Lovell Edgeworth in his *Memoirs*, Day was 'never more loved by any woman... nor do I believe, that any woman was to him ever personally more agreeable.' But Sabrina 'was too young and artless, to feel the extent of that importance, which my friend [*Day*] annexed to trifling concessions or resistance to fashion, particularly with respect to female dress.'

Day left Sabrina at a friend's house, along with some strict instructions on her mode of dress. Then disaster struck over a 'trifling circumstance... She did, or did not, wear certain long sleeves, and some handkerchief, which had been the object of his dislike, or of his liking.' Unfortunately Day equated her obedience to his wishes with proof of her attachment; disobedience proved 'her want of strength of mind.' So Thomas 'quitted her for ever!' He later married a Yorkshire heiress; Sabrina married a barrister.

'A CERTAIN STEP TOWARDS FALLING IN LOVE'

A dance at a ballroom or assembly is the best place to meet the opposite sex with propriety, under the watchful gaze of parents and chaperones. A young gentleman should learn how to dance *before* going to balls and assemblies – take dancing lessons if you haven't already learned at home. When you arrive at a ball, the master of ceremonies will give you a card with the dance steps on it, which is a useful reminder.

Don't step on your partner's toes – you will be laughed at, and it's not a good way to recommend yourself. Elizabeth Bennet is mortified at the Netherfield ball in *Pride and Prejudice*: 'Mr Collins, awkward and solemn, apologising instead of attending, and often moving wrong without being aware of it, gave her all the shame and misery which a disagreeable partner for a couple of dances can give. The moment of her release from him was ecstasy.'

Which dance steps should you learn? When Austen was a little girl in the early 1780s typical country dances included 'The Merry Meeting', 'The Liverpool Volunteers' and 'La Ville de Paris'.

Formerly, it was customary that a young lady stayed with the same dancing partner all evening. The next morning, the gentleman would call at her home and enquire after her health, but this custom had fallen into disuse by the time Jane attended balls.

English country dances and Scottish reels were danced at Almack's in 1814; the orchestra was conducted by the celebrated Neil Gow. The following year, Lady Jersey introduced a new dance from Paris, the quadrille. The first to dance the quadrille were Lady Jersey, Lady Harriet Butler, Lady Susan Ryde and Miss Montgomery, and their partners were the Count St Aldegonde, Mr Montgomery, Mr Montague, and Charles Standish. Jane Austen commented in a letter to her niece Fanny Knight that she thought quadrilles were 'pretty enough, though of course they are very inferior to the cotillions of my own day.'

The big question is, will you or won't you waltz? In this wildly successful but daring new dance, introduced at Almack's in about 1815, a lady must actually permit a young man to put his arm round her waist. Captain Gronow recalled: 'There were comparatively few who at first ventured to whirl round the *salons* of Almack's.' Young ladies should only waltz with a gentleman friend or one they've been introduced to, and they must not waltz at all before they are 'out'. When you waltz for the first time, it's initially alarming to feel the heat of a man's arm through your thin muslin gown. The poet Lord Byron, who knew a thing or two about seduction, disapproved of the 'lewd grasp, and lawless contact warm,' which the waltz's dancers enjoyed:

> *Endearing waltz, to thy more melting tune,*
> *Bow Irish jig- and ancient rigadoon,*
> *Scotch reels avaunt! and country dance forego,*
> *Your future claims to each fantastic toe,*
> *Waltz – Waltz – alone both arms and legs demands,*
> *Liberal of feet – and lavish of her hands,*
> *Hands which may freely range in public sight,*
> *Where ne'er before –but – pray "put out the light"...*
> ('Waltz', Lord George Gordon Byron, 1828)

But even the more prudish middle classes have fallen under the waltz's spell. In *Emma*, an impromptu dance begins at the party in Mr Cole's house, and Mrs Weston starts playing 'an irresistible waltz; and Frank Churchill, coming up with most becoming gallantry to Emma... secured her hand, and led her up to the top.'

You'll be dancing all night when in high society. The diplomat Sir George Jackson joked in a letter to his mother, (18 May 1808) that he had been up all night 'almost every day in the week' when staying in London. The previous night he went to a masked ball at Lady Buckingham's, then on to a supper, then 'quizzing, and dancing until six [*in the morning*], and I then walked home in my domino, which throughout the evening had been the admiration of everybody, and now afforded no small amusement to the milk-women, and the butchers and greengrocers going to market.' (A domino was a hooded cloak worn at masquerades).

Jane Austen loved dancing. In December 1798 she wrote to Cassandra about a ball at the Ashford Assembly Rooms. She'd been staying with her friend Catherine Bigg at Manydown. The behaviour of one gentleman present may have inspired Mr Darcy's standoffish conduct at the Meryton Assembly in *Pride and Prejudice*:

> I returned from Manydown this morning... Our ball was very thin, but by no means unpleasant... Mr Calland... appeared as usual with his hat in his hand, and stood every now and then behind Catherine and me to be talked to and abused for not dancing. We teased him, however, into it at last... There were twenty dances, and I danced them all, and without any fatigue... My black cap was openly admired.

If you live in the countryside, where there are fewer opportunities for a ball, you'll be thrilled when an impromptu dance takes place. In Austen's *Persuasion*, the Musgrove girls at the Great House in Uppercross, 'were wild for dancing; and the evenings ended, occasionally, in an unpremeditated little ball.' Fanny Price's first ball at *Mansfield Park* was 'the thought only of the afternoon, built on the late acquisition of a violin player in the servants' hall, and the possibility of raising five couple'. It was, however, 'a very happy one' for Fanny as she danced four times with her cousin Edmund.

'HEARTFELT DELIGHT'

A proposal of marriage is a delicate matter, and every gentleman has his own way of declaring his love. In *Pride and Prejudice*, Mr Darcy's proposal to Elizabeth Bennet is passionate but unflattering: 'In vain have I struggled. It will not do. My feelings will not be repressed. You must allow me to tell you how ardently I admire and love you.' But

Darcy does not recommend his suit when he declares that their marriage will be a 'degradation' and that he can hardly 'rejoice in the inferiority of your connections.' After a heated exchange Elizabeth angrily declares: 'You could not have made me the offer of your hand in any possible way that would have tempted me to accept it.'

So Elizabeth had a difficult task when accepting Mr Darcy's second proposal of marriage after so resolutely rejecting his first. She 'immediately, but not very fluently, gave him to understand, that her sentiments had undergone so material a change... as to make her receive with gratitude and pleasure his present assurances.'

How should you say 'Yes'? *Emma*'s Miss Woodhouse said 'Just what she ought, of course. A lady always does.' Once you have accepted a marriage proposal it's customary to ask your parents or guardian to approve the match. But as Jane Austen says in *Persuasion*: 'When any two young people take it into their heads to marry, they are pretty sure by perseverance to carry their point, be they ever so poor, or ever so imprudent, or ever so little likely to be necessary to each other's ultimate comfort.'

A gentleman and lady should not write to each other before they are engaged. *Sense and Sensibility*'s Elinor Dashwood is finally convinced that Lucy Steele has really been secretly engaged to Edward Ferrars for four years when Lucy produces his letters to her: 'a correspondence between them by letter could subsist only under a positive engagement, could be authorised by nothing else.'

Your parents may feel that a long engagement is inappropriate, even if your lover only has a small income at present, just in case something happens to prevent the marriage (as in Cassandra Austen's case). In *Persuasion*, Mr and Mrs Musgrove decide to let their daughter Henrietta marry Charles Hayter as quickly as possible 'and make the best of it', as it 'will be better than a long engagement.'

You can't set up home together unless you have enough to live on – but how much is 'enough'? It depends on your idea of domestic comforts. In *Sense and Sensibility* (1811) Elinor Dashwood's hoped-for future 'wealth' is a yearly income of £1,000 (roughly £67,000 today). Her extravagant sister Marianne's longed-for 'competence' of

£2,000 (approximately £134,000 p.a.) is the minimum needed to support a family with 'a proper establishment of servants, a carriage, perhaps two, and hunters.'

If clergyman Edward Ferrars had married the heiress Miss Morton, as John Dashwood points out, he would 'have been in receipt of two thousand five hundred a year... for Miss Morton has thirty thousand pounds.' When Edward decides to marry Elinor, his mother grudgingly gives him £10,000, which would generate interest of about £830 per year – when added to Elinor's 'fifty pounds a year', plus the Delaford living of £200 annually, this is rather more than the 'wealth' she hoped for, and is enough for them to live on.

WEDDING PREPARATIONS
A new set of clothes is essential for a bride. Mrs Allen tells Catherine in *Northanger Abbey* about the wedding of Miss Drummond, who was blessed with a large fortune: 'When she married, her father gave her twenty thousand pounds, and five hundred to buy wedding clothes.' In *Pride and Prejudice*, Mrs Bennet is horrified to learn that her husband refuses to 'advance a guinea' to buy wedding clothes for their errant daughter Lydia: 'She was more alive to the disgrace, which her want of new clothes must reflect on her daughter's nuptials, than to any sense of shame at her eloping and living with Wickham a fortnight before they took place.'

Your trousseau will be on display to the public before the wedding. In *Sense and Sensibility*, when the nuptials of Marianne Dashwood's faithless lover, Willoughby, and heiress Miss Grey are imminent, Mrs Palmer shows her 'sympathy' by telling Elinor: 'at what coach-maker's the new carriage was building, by what painter Mr Willoughby's portrait was drawn, and at what warehouse Miss Grey's clothes might be seen.'

It's customary to exchange gifts, perhaps some jewellery, with your family when you get married. In a letter dated 2 June 1805, Lady Elizabeth Foster, bosom friend of Georgiana, Duchess of Devonshire, detailed some of the presents given to Caroline Ponsonby for her marriage to William Lamb:

Caroline Ponsonby is to be married tomorrow; she looks prettier than ever I saw her. Sometimes she is very nervous, but... she appears quite happy. W. Lamb seems quite devoted to her. They supped here last night, and she received some presents and gave some. Lord Morpeth gave her a beautiful acqua marina [*sic*] clasp. I gave her a little pearl cross with a small diamond in the middle. Caroline gives a hair bracelet with amethyst clasp [*to me*]. Lord Melbourne gave her a beautiful set of amethysts, and Lady M. a diamond wreath. The Duke of Devonshire gives her her wedding gown, and the Duchess a beautiful veil.

> (Vere Foster, (ed.), *The Two Duchesses*,
> Blackie & Son Ltd, 1898).

Every bride-to-be dreams of a fabulous wedding dress, but of course it depends how much your parents can afford to spend. When heiress Miss Catherine Tilney Long married Mr Wellesley Pole in March 1812, *La Belle Assemblée* reported excitedly that the bride's dress: 'excelled, in costliness and beauty, the celebrated one worn by Lady Morpeth, at the time of her marriage, which was exhibited for a fortnight at least by her mother the late Duchess of Devonshire. The dress of the present bride consisted of a robe of real Brussel's [*sic*] point lace; the device a simple sprig; it was placed over white satin.'

Miss Long wore a cottage bonnet of Brussels lace with two ostrich feathers on her head: 'She likewise wore a deep lace veil, and a white satin pelisse, trimmed with swansdown. The dress cost 700 guineas; the bonnet 150; and the veil 200... The lady's jewels consist principally of a brilliant necklace and ear-rings; the former cost twenty-five thousand guineas.' Her bridegroom Wellesley 'wore a plain blue coat, with yellow buttons, a white waistcoat, and buff breeches, and white silk stockings'.

The day after the ceremony, the happy couple distributed over 800 silver wedding favours to their friends. The bride did not forget her domestic servants, including her old nurse; she settled lifetime annuities on them. Unfortunately for Miss Long, her immense fortune of £80,000 per annum was her principal attraction.

William proposed to her six times before she agreed to marry him; one account says that she finally consented in order to escape the Duke of Clarence's unwelcome attentions. Pole fought a duel with Lord Kilworth on her behalf, too. William took the name William Pole-Tilney-Long-Wellesley after the wedding.

Although they had three children together, the Wellesleys' married life was extremely unhappy. William spent Catherine's entire fortune, got into debt, took a mistress, and fled to France to escape his creditors. When Mrs Wellesley died (allegedly of a broken heart) on 12 September 1825, the *Gentleman's Magazine* noted that her marriage was 'not one of affection, but of importunity; that she yielded to a long and indefatigable siege; and not without the most pointed and daring threats, that the determined lover would not yield but with his life.'

Few weddings are as spectacular as Miss Long's, especially when the parties involved have 'no taste for finery or parade' like Emma Woodhouse and Mr Knightley in Austen's *Emma*. But if you have found 'perfect happiness', you'll cheerfully ignore the strictures of vulgar women like Mrs Elton who think that a wedding with 'very little white satin' and 'very few white veils' is a 'most pitiful business'.

BEGINNING MARRIED LIFE

The institution of marriage is regulated by Lord Hardwicke's Act of 1754. The banns must be read in church on three Sundays before the wedding takes place. Marriages must be solemnized in church before a clergyman. Alternatively, you can buy a special licence from a bishop or archbishop to dispense with banns. In *Pride and Prejudice*, when a delighted Mrs Bennet hears that her daughter Lizzie is engaged to Mr Darcy, she says: 'You must and shall be married by a special licence.'

High society belles may wed in a private ceremony at home. Princess Charlotte, the Prince Regent's only legitimate child, married Prince Leopold of Saxe-Coburg on 2 May 1816 in the great Crimson Drawing-Room at Carlton House.

When you have finally tied the knot, the family will inform the newspapers of your nuptials. As Jane Austen joked in a letter to Anna Lefroy after hearing that an acquaintance had recently married: 'I have never seen it in the papers, and one may as well be single if the wedding is not to be in print.' In *Sense and Sensibility*, Marianne Dashwood scours the papers every morning for news of Willoughby's wedding.

For your honeymoon, you may stay at a fashionable watering place like Buxton, Brighton or Margate, or one of the family's mansions. After Lord Byron married Miss Annabella Milbanke at her father Sir Ralph's house at Seaham in the county of Durham on 2 January 1815, they spent their honeymoon at Halnaby, another seat of Sir Ralph's in the same county.

The bride usually takes a female relative such as a sister with her on honeymoon. When Ann Wyatt married Daniel Vawdrey on 7 February 1804, her father Benjamin (brother of the famous architect James) gave her 'pocket money on her wedding - £50' and 'Lucy to accompany her £20.'

After the honeymoon you will begin married life in your own establishment at last (unless, like *Emma*'s Mr Knightley, you share your bride's parental home). As a new bride, you will be visited by your new neighbours, and should return their visits as soon as possible. You can now go out without a chaperone at last.

When Isabella Thorpe gets engaged to James Morland (*Northanger Abbey*), she looks forward to 'an honourable and speedy establishment... She saw herself, at the end of a few weeks, the gaze and admiration of every new acquaintance' and 'the envy of every valued old friend in Putney, with a carriage at her command, a new name on her tickets [*visiting cards*], and a brilliant exhibition of hoop rings on her finger.'

One of the advantages of being a bride is that you take precedence over the other ladies. At the Crown in *Emma*, Miss Woodhouse: 'must submit to stand second to Mrs Elton, even though she had always considered the ball peculiarly for her. It was almost enough to make her think of marrying.' A bride also takes precedence over her unmarried sisters, like Lydia Wickham in *Pride and Prejudice*: 'Ah, Jane, I take your place now, and you must go lower, because I am a married woman.'

Once married, your 'first object' must be your 'husband's happiness', because your own is linked with it, according to Mrs William Parkes' *Domestic Duties* (1825). You will have new duties to perform, too. Before your marriage, you are unlikely to have had any major financial responsibilities, except keeping within your allowance from your parents or guardian. Now you are responsible for running a household, managing servants, and doing charitable work locally. When 19-year-old Marianne Dashwood marries Colonel Brandon in *Sense and Sensibility*, she finds herself 'placed in a new home, a wife, the mistress of a family, and the patroness of a village' at Delaford.

Unless your new partner is blessed with robust health, your first marriage is unlikely to be your only one. Second and third marriages are quite common: Jane Austen's brothers James, Henry, Frank and Charles all married twice. As we shall see in the final chapter, childbirth is a very dangerous time for women.

These are perilous days, too, because of the 'great war'. If your husband is in the army or navy, then you face great anxiety when they are on active service, like *Persuasion*'s Anne Elliot. She 'gloried in being a sailor's wife, but she must pay the tax of quick alarm for belonging to that profession.'

The horrors of the French Revolution robbed Jane's cousin of her first husband. Eliza Hancock married a French aristocrat, the Comte de Feuillide; he died on the guillotine in 1794. The pleasure-loving Eliza was a lonely widow and about a year after the Comte's death, she refused a proposal from Henry Austen; Eliza was ten years older than her youthful suitor. Sometime in the mid-1790s James Austen, who had recently been widowed, proposed to Eliza as well. But life in a quiet country parsonage did not attract Eliza, who liked a busy social life, and she turned him down. Then in 1797 Henry proposed again and this time was accepted.

RUNAWAYS
What if you meet the partner of your dreams but your parents or guardian object to their character, age, family connections or lack of

fortune? If you are not willing to wait, and are underage, your lover may ask you to elope to Gretna Green and marry them anyway.

The marriages of minors (people under 21) who wed without their parents' consent are not legal, even with a special licence. But Hardwicke's Act does not apply to Scotland: there it is legal for people as young as 16 to marry without parental consent. The village of Gretna Green lies temptingly just over the Scottish border, and it is the first destination of choice for hundreds of runaway marriages.

Fortune hunters are always in search of rich brides. In *Pride and Prejudice*, inexperienced teenager Georgiana Darcy falls easy prey to Wickham's charm, as Mr Darcy tells Elizabeth Bennet: 'Georgiana.. was persuaded to believe herself in love, and to consent to an elopement... Mr Wickham's chief object was unquestionably my sister's fortune, which is thirty thousand pounds.' But Georgiana could not bear to hurt her brother's feelings and told him of their plans. He took swift action to protect her.

The newspapers regularly report elopements such as that of a nobleman and a banker's daughter. In May 1782 John Fane, 10th Earl of Westmorland (1759–1841), ran away with Sarah-Anne Child, the only offspring of the fabulously wealthy Robert Child of Osterley Park, Middlesex. The earl met the young lady at a fashionable resort, but his courtship was rejected by her parents, who wanted Sarah-Anne to marry a nobleman of higher fortune. According to Robert Elliot's *Gretna Green Memoirs* (1842), Mr Child told the earl: 'Your blood is good, my lord, but money is better.'

But Sarah-Anne was completely won over by her noble lover's addresses, and in the early hours of 17 May 1782, she tiptoed past her sleeping governess. Then, accompanied by her favourite maidservant, Sarah-Anne crept out of her father's London home in Berkeley Square. The earl met them with a chaise-and-four and they galloped off towards Scotland.

The alarm was soon raised and Mr and Mrs Child set off in hot pursuit, but after several stages, they discovered that the earl had cunningly bespoken all the fresh horses. Robert Elliot's version of the story, (written some years after the event) claimed that Mr Child shot and killed one of the earl's horses to try and stop him, but the earl's servant cut the leather suspension on the banker's chaise, and Child was unable to catch the lovers.

John and Sarah-Anne successfully reached Gretna Green and were married on 20 May. Their union seems to have been a happy one until Sarah-Anne's death in 1793; they had a son and three daughters. But if the earl banked on getting his hands on the Child fortune, he was outfoxed by the bride's enraged father, who vowed that no earl of Westmorland would get a penny of his money. When Robert Child died, the bulk of his property and fortune went to the runaway couple's eldest daughter, Sarah Sophia Fane. (This lady later became Lady Jersey, famous patroness of Almack's).

A young lady fed up with a restricted home life may jump at the chance to run away. Heiress Augusta Nicholson showed great ingenuity in the autumn of 1809 when love came a-calling in the handsome form of John Giles, a penniless comedian.

Miss Nicholson, a ward of chancery, stood to inherit £14,000 when she came of age, owing to the deaths of no less than eight relatives in the previous six years. Augusta's mother was dead, and her father Col Nicholson had remarried. It's said that Augusta did not get on well with her stepmother, Mrs Nicholson.

While her father was away, Miss Nicholson and her stepmother visited the fashionable resort of Tunbridge Wells. One day Augusta went to the library. She happened to meet Giles there (he may have planned it beforehand) and he gallantly offered to carry her library books home for her. A whirlwind romance began. The very next evening Augusta and her stepmother went to the theatre to watch Giles perform, and sat in one of the boxes close to the stage. Unnoticed by her unsuspecting stepmother, Augusta threw a letter to Giles in which she 'acknowledged her attachment to him, and gave him encouragement to pay her addresses to her, and said that she would marry him' (*Annual Register for the Year 1809*).

When Mrs Nicholson discovered Giles was paying court to her stepdaughter, she banned her from going out. Nothing daunted, Augusta and Giles began a clandestine correspondence: he smuggled letters to her through the front door keyhole. And every morning for five weeks, Augusta got up before five o'clock and chatted to her lover from her bedroom window.

The lovers were desperate to elope, but Giles 'was destitute of the most needful article, money, for carrying on such an exploit' so he borrowed £30 from a fellow thespian, Mr Smith. In November 1809 Smith and Giles hired a chaise-and-four and Smith looked after the carriage while Giles rescued Augusta. They fled to London, and eventually found lodgings in Westmorland Place. Augusta made Giles repeatedly swear on the Bible that he would never marry anyone else.

A wedding ring was purchased and the banns for their marriage read twice at Marylebone Church, when the runaways were tracked down by the Nicholson family solicitor: 'A frantic tragic scene took place... both lovers rushed into each other's arms, and swore attachment, beating their heads, and running about the room distracted.' But the game was up and the lovers were parted. Giles and Smith were now in real hot water because Augusta was a ward of court, and the Court of Chancery began proceedings against them. Despite his protestations that he did not know Augusta was a ward of court, Giles was committed to the Fleet Prison for a time.

At last Augusta got her wish: she married John the following spring, and they had a little boy. If Giles *had* married Augusta for her money, initially it seemed he was doomed to disappointment because his wife died shortly before she came of age. The estate went to her brother but he died before taking control of the property, and so Giles and Augusta's son became heir to her fortune. If it was truly a love match, Augusta's death was a tragic finale to the comedian's courtship.

CHAPTER 7

In Sickness and in Health

*'Oh, I am not at all afraid of her dying. People do not
die of little trifling colds.'*
(Jane Austen, *Pride and Prejudice*, 1813)

If you've visited England before, then you'll know that even very genteel folk are often unacquainted with the use of soap. The *London Magazine* (October 1775) complained that ladies' gowns were used 'to hide dirt and avoid cleanliness.' Now, magazines such as *La Belle Assemblée* (February 1806), recommend that ladies wash regularly and wear: 'Linen, always white, which never betrays the inevitable effect of perspiration and of dust; a skin ever clean and brilliant; garments unsoiled by any stain, and which might be taken for the robes of a nymph; a shoe which appears as if though it had never touched the ground.'

'Cleanliness' in your toilette 'has the greatest merit in the eyes of the delicate [*fastidious*] man,' *La Belle Assemblée* reiterated in December 1806. 'Cleanliness alone... has a right to please, to attract the eye, to gratify the taste, to excite desire.' The writer warns that 'the girl of fifteen who strives not to please, will be a shrew and a slut at twenty-five.'

As we saw earlier, soap is taxed, so it is expensive. Middlewood's 'Royal Abyssinian Flower Soap... will wash the hands and face beautifully clean, white and smooth' also 'rendering shaving pleasant to the tenderest face.' It cost '1s the square', according to an advertisement in *La Belle Assemblée* (November, 1807).

Those fine ladies who find daily washing inconvenient can buy lavender water, extract of violets, or 'otto of roses' to mask their odour. According to his diary, when James Harris, 1st Earl of Malmesbury was delegated to bring Princess Caroline of Brunswick to Britain in 1795 to marry the Prince of Wales, she was so careless about her personal hygiene that she was 'offensive' to the nose. When the Prince of Wales met Caroline for the first time, he was so appalled that he gallantly exclaimed: 'Harris, I am not well; pray get me a glass of brandy.'

As well as perfume you can buy beauty aids like face creams, lotions and rouge from the perfumer's shop. It is no longer fashionable to paint your face and neck as lavishly as in the last century, though. When *Persuasion*'s vain baronet, Sir Walter Elliot, compliments his daughter Anne on her 'improved looks', he asks if she has been using Gowland's lotion and is surprised to hear she has not used anything for her complexion.

But Gowland's lotion, costing 5s 6d per pint (568ml) in 1807, contains an extract of bitter almonds and a compound of mercury. A writer in *La Belle Assemblée* (April 1806) lamented the use of 'dangerous applications of paints and washes... composed of the most pernicious materials.' The *Belfast Monthly Magazine* (March 1812) reported that cosmetics such as carmine (rouge) for lips and cheeks contain insidious poisons like lead and mercury, and females 'generally fall early victims to their own indiscretion.' Cold cream or 'pommad divin' at first gives the skin an 'angelic whiteness', but it soon acquires a 'dirty brown' hue.

Some ladies use 'pearl powder' to whiten their face, neck and bosom, and this preparation may contain bismuth. If a lady wearing pearl powder made from bismuth ventures into a room lit by gaslight, the pigment undergoes a chemical reaction and her skin turns as black as coal!

It is not necessary to resort to these noxious potions; try washing your face with milk or astringent Hungary water made from rosemary leaves and flowers. A blooming complexion unaided by dubious cosmetics is safest. *La Belle Assemblée* (April 1806) warned its fair readers that the 'made-up beauty' lives in 'continual terror of some unlucky accident, which may discover her shape to be owing to the skill of a stay-maker, her teeth to that of a dentist, her hair to be only a fashionable wig, and her complexion bought at a perfumer's!'

'A TOOTH AMISS'

A beautiful smile is very attractive, so brush your teeth well; if not your black teeth and bad breath will drive away your lovers. Tooth-powder is made from a variety of substances such as charcoal (the finest is made from 'cocoa-nut' shells). Some people use 'powder of burnt bread', recommended by Dr Cook as the 'best and safest' of dentifrices. 'Ashes of tobacco... make the teeth white,' but are deemed 'too indelicate' for ladies' use (*Lady's Magazine*, September 1775).

Teeth and gum problems are common to all ranks of society. An eighteenth century receipt book owned by Mrs Owen of Lancashire includes a recipe for tooth powder using myrrh and cream of tartar. The same book recommends rinsing one's gums several times a day with a mixture of sage tea and red wine as a useful cure for scurvy.

Around 1777, Lady Newdigate (neé Hester Margaretta Mundy) wrote to her husband Sir Roger, who was staying at London, to ask him to buy some sarsaparilla: 'I wish you would get me some Sassiperella [*sic*] (I don't know whether I spell it right). I mean ye herb dried; it is given as an anti-Scorbutic, whether sold at the Herb shops or Apothecaries I know not.'

When using a toothbrush make sure that the bristles are secure, or you may suffer the same fate as one unfortunate lady. The *Gentleman's Magazine* (August 1792) reported that Mrs Pitt of Cirencester 'was cleaning her teeth with a brush, some of the hairs of which, being loose... slipped into her throat, and by the irritation they caused, brought on a violent fit of coughing and vomiting, which, in her advanced state of pregnancy, produced the most dismal consequences, and she survived the accident but one day.'

Samuel and Sarah Adams' *The Complete Servant* includes instructions to ladies' maids on how to make a toothbrush. First, fresh marshmallow roots are carefully dried, then the ends bruised with a mallet until they form a brush. The brush is then dyed and hardened in a heated mixture of dragons' blood (tree resin) and conserve of roses.

A toothpick will help keep your teeth clean after meals. Toothpicks are made from goose quills, or ivory, or precious metals like gold and silver; you'll need a case to carry them with you. Margaret Pedder paid 7s 6d for an ivory toothpick case when passing through Birmingham in the 1780s.

Toothpick cases are a good way to show off your wealth. In *Sense and Sensibility*, the Dashwood sisters are detained for some time at Gray's (a jeweller) in Sackville Street while gentleman Robert Ferrars hesitates over choosing the decoration of a case:

> At last the affair was decided. The ivory, the gold, and the pearls, all received their appointment; and the gentleman having named the last day on which his existence could be continued without the possession of the toothpick-case, drew on his gloves with leisurely care and ... walked off with a happy air of real conceit and affected indifference.

If you have toothache, Samuel and Sarah Adams' *Complete Servant* recommends 'Washing behind the ears with cold water every morning' as an 'infallible' remedy; alternatively they suggest inserting a red-hot wire into the hollow of your decayed tooth to kill the nerve.

Mrs Owen of Lancashire's remedy for toothache was a handful of sage, an ounce-and-a-half of honey, 2 scruples of Roman vitriol (copper sulphate), and a drachm of alum. The sage leaves were boiled in 3 pints of water until the liquid was reduced by half, then the chemicals were dissolved in the solution. The sufferer rinsed the mouth with the medicine, then spat it out again; the recipe was also said to be 'a great preservative of ye teeth.' A note on the page comments that 'Blistering behind the neck, betwixt ye shoulders, is very good for the tooth ach [*sic*].'

If these sure-fire remedies do not work, and you still have a 'tooth amiss', like Harriet Smith in *Emma*, consult a dentist (if in town) or a 'tooth-drawer'. Local barbers will pull out rotting teeth, too. But if staying in the countryside, you may have to resort to the local blacksmith to extract your teeth.

Even if you brush your teeth diligently, unless you are very lucky you'll have lost several teeth by middle age. When Jane Austen's cousin Philadelphia Walter met the Austens at a family gathering in 1788, she wrote to her brother: 'My aunt has lost several fore-teeth, which makes her look old.' Jane's mother was then about 49 years old.

If you have lost some teeth you can buy a set of the new 'mineral' (porcelain) teeth from France. M. Faleur of Russell Square advertised his 'improved mineral teeth' in *La Belle Assemblée* (August 1807): 'Their effect will prove so beneficial as to answer every purpose of mastication; and their appearance so natural as to impose on the critical observer.' Or your dentist may equip you with 'Waterloo teeth': dentures of human teeth extracted from soldiers' bodies strewn across the battlefield. Teeth are also harvested from corpses (the fresher the better) supplied by the 'resurrection men'.

'Resurrection men', as grave robbers are jocularly known, illegally dig up freshly buried corpses from graveyards to supply surgeons with bodies so that they can practise their dissection skills. Their depredations are notorious and watchmen are employed to guard churchyards overnight.

In 1819 one unfortunate constable, Mr Baker of Wallington, discovered the body of his recently deceased sister in a horse and cart; he had buried her only the day before (*The Times*, 28 January 1819). Later that year *The Times* (22 April) reported that a bank clerk, Thomas Johnson of Reigate, was very distressed when he discovered that his infant son, interred the previous month, was one of several bodies stolen by resurrection men Joseph Naples and George Marden.

If your friends have rotten teeth, or are addicted to snuff-taking, you may find it hard to maintain a polite front when almost suffocated by their halitosis. But if *you* suffer from bad breath, try this 'radical remedy' from *The Family Oracle of Health* (1824): 'Take from five to ten drops of muriatic [*hydrochloric*] acid, in an ale glassful of barley water, and add a little lemon juice and lemon peel to flavour. Mix for a draught, to be taken three times a day, for a month or six weeks... if effectual, it may be continued occasionally.'

MAKING A SPECTACLE OF YOURSELF

During the eighteenth century it was fashionable to wear spectacles. They were thought to give wearers an air of wisdom as they were assumed to have worn out their eyes from long study. The lenses were taken out of the spectacle frames if unnecessary to improve the wearer's vision.

The *Spirit of the Public Journals for 1801* (1802) commented:

> Formerly no person, young or old, man or woman, could appear in public without spectacles. They did not wear them for the purpose of aiding their sight; for when asked to read anything, they requested permission to take off their spectacles. Today the young people who wear glasses wish at least to escape the fatigues of war, by pretending to be short-sighted.

Don't spend too long reading by candlelight if you want to preserve your sight. Spectacles cost from 1s to over a guinea, depending on the cost of the materials; some are made with silver. In Austen's *Emma*, Miss Bates is immensely grateful when Frank Churchill offers to fasten the rivet of her mother's spectacles: '"Oh", said he! "I do think I can fasten the rivet; I like a job of this kind excessively".'

KILL OR CURE

Death and disease is all around you. Jane Austen's sister-in-law Eliza, James's wife, died in May 1795 less than 24 hours after becoming ill. If you become unwell during your stay, medical practitioners are listed in the local town directory, although you may prefer to ask your friends and neighbours if they can recommend one.

But be warned, a physician's services may send you to an early grave. Medicine is still an evolving science – its practitioners do not understand the underlying causes of diseases such as smallpox, 'consumption' (tuberculosis), measles, etc. Nor do they understand the necessity for washing their hands when visiting a patient. The poorest people go to public hospitals when ill but these establishments are repositories of filth and contagion.

Only wealthy people can afford to have a physician in attendance. Physicians are university-educated and chiefly based in London. A 'licentiate' (trained at Edinburgh or perhaps on the continent) is slightly cheaper but still too pricey for most middle class families, who usually resort to an apothecary. Apothecaries prepare medicines in accordance with a physician's directions, but they also prescribe for patients, especially if no other medical man is available in the area.

Surgeons can prescribe medicines as well as perform surgical procedures. They are now far more knowledgeable than in earlier times, thanks to the foundation of schools of anatomy, and in 1800 George III granted a Royal charter to the College of Surgeons of England. Medicine is now a highly respectable middle class profession. In March 1812 Mrs Jackson wrote to her son Sir George:

> Mr Creaser, our favourite Bath medical practitioner, gave a magnificent dinner last week. [*One*] gentleman... supposed Mr Creaser should be very rich, for the dinner was such as he should have expected from a man of £7,000 or £8,000 a year – claret, champagne, etc. Mrs C. had a party in the evening and it was really a good one – full of diamonds.
> (Lady Jackson, (ed.), *The Bath Archives*, 1873).

The chief treatments available have been widely used for many years: blood letting, applying leeches to the affected part, 'cupping', 'blistering', and emetics and purges such as rhubarb or Glauber's salts. Any or all of these together are employed when a person is poorly. In 'cupping' a taper is lit inside a cup, to consume the air inside; the cup is then applied to the skin, and the suction created is thought to relieve pressure inside the body.

For example, John Perkins' *Every Woman Her Own House-Keeper* (1796) recommends the following for a headache:

> Bleeding is necessary... to be repeated if there be any occasion. Cupping also, or the application of leeches to the temples or behind the ears, will be of service. Afterwards a blistering plaster [*which inflamed the skin*] may be applied to the neck... in some cases it will be necessary to blister the whole head... The body ought likewise to be kept open by gentle laxatives.

If you are afflicted by worms, Perkins suggests a strong purgative such as calomel (a compound of mercury) or tincture of senna, with 'a glass of good wine'. Or you could try the medicine sold at a London shop; Robert Southey saw its stomach-churning window display: 'Here you have a collection of worms from the human intestines, curiously bottled, and every bottle with a label stating to whom the worm belonged, and testifying that the party was relieved from it by virtue of the medicine which is sold within.'

Take great care not to get too chilled or overheated, as even a seemingly trivial complaint like a cold may prove fatal. In his *Memoirs*, George Elers recalled that his friend George Wenyeve of Brettenham Park 'caught his death' after becoming overheated 'while shooting one very hot day in September... he caught a violent cold and nearly lost the use of his limbs, and died about 1812.'

Emma's egregious Mr Elton is alarmed on Miss Woodhouse's behalf when her friend Harriet has a bad sore throat: 'A sore throat! – I hope not infectious. I hope not of a putrid infectious sort. Has Perry seen her? Indeed you should take care of yourself as well as of your friend. Let me entreat you to run no risks.'

You should have your family and servants inoculated against smallpox; in 1776 Parson Woodforde paid for his servants to be inoculated. This dreadful disease kills thousands yearly – around one in four people who catch it will perish. Smallpox survivors are often left horribly disfigured by scars (which account for many ladies' addiction to skin creams and paints) or even blinded.

In the early eighteenth century, Lady Mary Wortley Montagu popularised the practice of inoculation ('variolation') in England. If a person was deliberately infected with smallpox through the skin, they caught a mild form of the disease, after which they were largely immune. However, the procedure is risky: some people die afterwards. Emily Elizabeth Fox, daughter of Stephen Fox (2nd Baron Holland) died in 1772 after being inoculated when she was just a few months old. It is considered safer to wait until children are at least three years old before inoculating them.

The big breakthrough against smallpox came in 1796 when Dr Edward Jenner (1749–1823) experimented on a boy named Phipps. Jenner showed that if a person was 'vaccinated' with cowpox (*variolae* vaccine) they were mostly safe from smallpox. So caring parents ensure that their children are protected against smallpox, in spite of their fears. Fanny D'Arblay (née Burney) was terrified when her little boy Alex was vaccinated in March 1797. The surgeon, Dr Ansel, gave him a lump of barley sugar to suck on while he underwent the 'dreaded' procedure. Alex was very brave, and his mother extremely proud of her 'little hero'.

Opiates such as highly addictive laudanum are available for pain relief for patients of all ages, even babies. Jane Austen's mother occasionally took laudanum drops to help her sleep when feeling unwell. Peruvian bark or quinine is used to treat many complaints including fevers, scrofula and consumption.

But no anaesthesia is available if your medical attendant insists that a surgical operation is necessary. The poet Thomas Moore had a recurring problem with an abscess in his side. In April 1806 he underwent an operation to stitch it up, which took two hours. He wrote to his mother to say that the procedure 'has given me more pain than I have [*ever*] felt yet, and will confine me for about eight days.' Laudanum is sometimes given to ease the pain during the operation or afterwards, depending on the procedure.

If you have suffered a major compound fracture of a limb, or it is so diseased that major ulceration or mortification has set in, your surgeon will recommend amputation if he believes your life is at risk. The author of the *Edinburgh Practice of Physic and Surgery* (1800) boasted:

> No part of surgery is brought to greater perfection than the manner of performing amputation. Before the invention of the tourniquet, and the method of securing the vessels by ligature, the operation was seldom undertaken; and a great proportion of those upon whom it was performed died soon after. In the present improved method, one death does not happen in twenty, or even thirty cases.

If you have to undergo amputation, several attendants will hold your limb steady. First the surgeon will make some incisions to create a flap of skin to cover the limb's stump after removal. Then he will saw off your limb as expeditiously as possible. It will be advantageous to the surgeon as well as yourself if you lose consciousness during the procedure so that your screams do not disturb his concentration.

Diseases like cancer are very difficult to treat. Jane Austen's aunt Philadelphia Hancock suffered a lingering, agonising death from breast cancer in 1792. Philadelphia's daughter Eliza (wife of Jane's brother Henry) became ill in 1813, and her death that year may be owing to the same disease.

The novelist Madame D'Arblay (Fanny Burney) was more fortunate. In her journal she recalled her 'dreadful operation' to remove her breast in 1811, owing to the 'menace of cancer.' The operation was performed by the celebrated surgeon Baron de Larrey.

QUACK CURES

If you are staying in the countryside, the nearest physician may be miles away, or he may lack specialist knowledge, so people try home remedies when ill. Parson Woodforde recorded in his diary (14 April 1781): 'I put a rosted [*sic*] onion in my Ear going to bed to night [*sic*]' for the 'throbbing pain' in his ear.

If folk remedies don't work, and you are unwilling to submit to a physician's tender mercies, you may be tempted to try the pills and medicines advertised in newspapers and magazines. Some of these quack doctors' nostrums are highly dangerous. An anonymous *Essay on Quackery* (1805) reported the death from poisoning of a little boy at Hull in December 1803 following a dose of 'Ching's Patent Worm Destroying Lozenges', which contained mercury.

John Corry, in his *Satirical View of London* (1815), expostulates: 'Cures, little less than miraculous, are *said* to be daily performed by the administration of nostrums, such as De Velno's Vegetable Syrup'. Men like 'Doctors Brodum, Solomon and Senate' grow rich and live in 'a style of grandeur' from peddling their 'mixtures of treacle, water and a variety of nauseous ingredients.' Dr Senate's chief claim to fame are his 'Lozenges of steel', allegedly a cure for impotence.

If the 'lozenges of steel' prove lacklustre in their results, and your efforts to start a family have not yet been blessed with success, you could spend the night in Dr Graham's celebrated 'Celestial Bed'. The bed, 'for the use of married people only,' is situated at the doctor's 'Temple of Hymen', a sumptuously decorated mansion in Pall Mall. He charges a hefty 50 guinea fee.

As Dr Graham ingeniously explains in his *Medical transactions at the Temple of health in London in ... 1780*: 'The CELESTIAL BED is highly electrified, so that the persons basking therein bask in a genial, invigorating tide of the celestial fire; which, as it powerfully vivifies, at the same time it removes all impediments; it cannot fail in the nature of things of producing a healthy and most beauteous offspring.' The good doctor also has a 'Temple of Health' at the Royal Terrace, Adelphi, where the public may purchase his 'Three great medicines – Electrical Aether, Nervous Aethereal Balsam, and Imperial Pills!' Incredible to relate, the doctor claims that the 'Electrical Aether' cannot be beaten for its prevention of all types of 'malignant or infectious disease' and for curing all 'nervous and putrid disorders.'

CHILDBIRTH AND CHILDREN

If you are expecting a baby, you will be feeling anxious. At this time a wife's most important duty is giving her husband children, but it's also her most perilous one. Even if she survives the child's birth, infection and fever often set in shortly afterwards.

Jane Austen's mother was extremely fortunate to survive eight pregnancies. When Jane's sister-in-law Mary's (James's second wife) first baby was imminent, Jane wrote to Cassandra: 'I believe I never told you that Mrs Coulthard and Anne, late of Manydown, are both dead, and both in childbed. We have not regaled Mary with this news.' Fortunately Mary's little boy James Edward was born safely, and mother and child were well.

However, three of Jane Austen's sister-in-laws lost their lives during or just after childbirth. Edward Austen's wife Elizabeth (née Bridges) died in October 1808, a few days after the birth of a little boy. The couple married in 1791; Elizabeth was only 35, and had already had 10 children before her last fatal confinement. Charles's wife Fanny was next. She died in 1814 shortly after the birth of a baby girl. Nearly a decade later, Frank Austen's wife Mary died in 1823 when their eleventh child was born; a hauntingly similar tragedy to that of his brother Edward's wife Elizabeth.

Most well-to-do women give birth at home, as public hospitals are riddled with infection, with several patients crammed into each bed. When women believe their baby is due, they arrange for the local physician to attend, or alternatively a 'man midwife' or *accoucheur,* often aided by a local midwife. According to the Machell family of Lancashire's accounts, in April 1775 Mr Machell paid Dr Fell three guineas for attending his wife during her lying-in, and paid 10s 6d to 'Jane Jackson midwife'.

Even the most expensive medical care could not save Princess Charlotte, the heir to the throne and the nation's darling. The whole country was plunged into mourning when she died on 6 November 1817, the day after the birth of her first child, a stillborn little boy. The 22-year-old princess had endured a lengthy and exhausting labour over two days. Her *accoucheur* Sir Richard Croft was overwhelmed with guilt, and later committed suicide.

It was formerly fashionable for genteel women to employ wet nurses. All Mrs Austen's children were put out to nurse locally until they were about two years old. However, Richard Reece's *Medical Guide* (1828) recommended that mothers should nurse their own children whenever possible, as 'no other woman's milk can be so good for her child.' But if this was not possible for some reason, the new mother should choose a 'clean, healthy, sober and temperate' wet nurse.

Repeated pregnancies may lead to health problems. Breastfeeding is thought to have a contraceptive effect, so some women prefer to nurse their babies themselves. But women of genteel birth find it difficult to limit the number of their pregnancies unless they sleep in a separate bedroom to their husband. *La Belle Assemblée* (August 1807) included an advertisement by J.P. Heath of Nottingham for 'Essence of pennyroyal' at 1s 1½d per bottle; it was sold to ladies purportedly to cure 'irregularities' in their menstrual cycle.

Child mortality is extremely high. Reece estimated that 'one half of the children of this country die before they are eight years old.' Babies and children are at risk from diseases such as smallpox, whooping cough, scarlet fever, measles, etc. On 18 March 1791 Woodforde wrote in his diary: 'I buried a poor infant of Henry Bakers [*sic*] this Even' a Girl, who died in the Small-pox, aged 1 year. The poor Infant had the... Small-pox, besides having at the same time the whooping-Cough, and also cutting teeth, her Name was Anne.'

Keeping your child clean may help prevent disease. In her *Domestic Duties: Or Instructions to Young Married Ladies* (1825), Mrs William Parkes recommends that children are washed daily with a sponge and 'abundance of cold water from head to foot.' This 'wholesome and bracing habit' should be supplemented with a weekly bath in a tub of warm water.

DEATH AND MOURNING

As death is never far away in Austen's England, during your stay you'll almost certainly need to buy some mourning wear. When you stroll along the street, or travel in your curricle, it's so commonplace to see a funeral procession that few people bother to turn their heads as the carriages slowly trundle past. Traveller Louis Simond commented: 'Their solemnity forms... a sad and a ridiculous contrast with the light and rapid motion of the carriages of the living, splashing them as they drive by... Some of the friends of the deceased follow in their carriages.'

Simond witnessed the funeral of a lady who lived in an upper storey of his Edinburgh lodgings in the early 1800s. The lady was not wealthy but was given a dignified send-off in a: 'Coach and six, covered with black cloth, and surmounted with plumes of feathers of the same colour, followed by more carriages, with a number of hired mourners on foot, before and behind, in black, and carrying likewise black plumes of feathers.'

A splendid funeral procession is another way of displaying one's wealth and status as well as marking one's grief. After Princess Charlotte died, her body was taken from Claremont to lie in state at Windsor. The church bells tolled and the road was lined with mournful crowds paying their last respects to their beloved princess. The solemn procession was led by a hearse carrying her baby's remains, and an urn containing the princess's heart. Next came Princess Charlotte's hearse pulled by eight black horses, and followed by five mourning carriages, two with six horses, the others with four black horses.

When you have lost a loved one, it's customary to wear mourning, and to buy suitable mourning for your servants, too. Not everyone agrees on how long mourning should last, and customs vary from place to place. There are three stages of mourning: full (or deep), second mourning, and half-mourning. It's usual to wear full mourning for close relatives such as parents, spouse, grandparents and siblings.

When the king's daughter Princess Amelia died, *Walker's Hibernian Magazine* (November 1786) gave general advice: 'A wife mourns for her husband, a year and six weeks; four months and a half in cambrick [*sic*], the cloak, gown and petticoat of French stuff, four months and a half in crape and woollen, three months in silk and gauze, and six weeks in half-mourning.'

Black bombazine (a wool and silk fabric) is a suitable material for gowns, and black caps and veils are worn; flashy jewellery and diamonds are put away until mourning is over. It's acceptable to wear a brooch or ring set with a lock of the deceased's hair, however.

For a husband who has lost his wife, the whole mourning period is far shorter – just six months. Men wear black crape hatbands and white 'weepers': pieces of muslin stitched onto coat sleeves. Jane Austen joked in a letter to Cassandra (17 May 1799) that she had recently met Dr Hall, who was 'in such very deep mourning that either his mother, his wife or himself must be dead.' In *Emma*, when Frank Weston Churchill's aunt (and adopted mother) Mrs Churchill dies, he cannot marry Jane Fairfax as soon as he had hoped, because as she says: 'There must be three months, at least, of deep mourning.' And Frank's father Mr Weston resolves 'that his mourning should be as handsome as possible.'

Full mourning is followed by 'second' mourning: black and white articles of clothing are now permissible. For half-mourning, sombre-hued fabrics like mauve and grey are allowed; men wear black gloves and perhaps a black crape hatband. Half-mourning is worn to show respect for the death of more distant relations, even estranged ones. *Persuasion*'s Elizabeth Elliot wears 'black ribands' for the recently deceased wife of the Kellynch estate's heir-presumptive, Mr Elliot, even though the family has not had any contact with him for 'several years'.

Children wear mourning, too. When Jane's brother Edward Knight lost his first wife Elizabeth, two of their children, George and Edward, stayed with Jane at Castle Square in Southampton for a few days. Both boys were anxious to have the correct clothing. Their other aunt Mrs James Austen had bought them a suit of mourning clothes, but their aunt Jane ordered more to be made up, as she explained in a letter to Cassandra (24 October 1808): 'Edward has an old black coat, which will save *his* [*sic*] having a second new one; but I find that black pantaloons are regarded by them as necessary, and of course one would not have them made uncomfortable by the want of what is usual on such occasions.'

When an important member of the Royal family dies like Princess Charlotte, you'll have to buy suitable mourning for that occasion, too, which really irks domestic economists like Fanny Price's stingy Aunt Norris in *Mansfield Park*. The Hon. Amelia Murray remembered that while she was at school with Lord Eldon's daughter: 'At the time of a Court mourning, I saw the piece of red tape which the Lord Chancellor himself enclosed in a letter to his daughter, telling her to measure carefully the length of her petticoat, that there might be no unnecessary waste in the quantity of bombazine to be sent!'

TAKING THE WATERS

Hope springs eternal, and if you are ill or convalescent your physician will recommend that you 'take the waters' at one of the many fashionable spas such as Bath, Buxton, Cheltenham, Tunbridge Wells, Harrogate, and Bristol's 'hot wells'. Modern medical practitioners will assure you that drinking and bathing in mineral water relieves many ailments like gout, rheumatism, and the palsy. Your doctor may give you a special diet to follow, and prescribe blood-letting in addition to taking the waters.

The city of Bath, with its warm mineral springs, is still a famous holiday and health resort, although its popularity has been overtaken by Brighton. Bath has its own social 'season' in the winter months, with a less popular season in late spring.

Bath is renowned for its cream-coloured buildings of freestone. In the mid-eighteenth century John Wood the elder and his son created elegant streets like the Circus and Royal Crescent. In August 1791 novelist Fanny Burney (later Madame D'Arblay) went to Bath to recover her health. Fanny wrote in her diary: 'It looks a city of palaces, a town of hills, and a hill of towns,' and she thought that the white stones of its buildings made it look 'beautiful and wonderful throughout.' But *Persuasion*'s Anne Elliot found the 'white glare' of the city in September oppressive.

The four public baths are open-air and surrounded by handsome colonnades to shelter bathers from the weather. The celebrated King's, Queen's, Hot, and Cross-Bath are frequented by the common sort. Men and women bathe together, and you'll see people entering the water with running sores and open ulcers. Poor people pay 6d for bathing. Genteel folk now resort to Bath Corporation's private baths on Stall Street, adjoining the King's Bath, and the Abbey Baths belonging to Earl Manvers. You pay 3s for the private bath; the fee includes bathing-dresses and towels. If you don't want to immerse your whole body the 'dry-pump' can direct water on the affected limb using a pump supplied by the spring.

A sedan chair is the most convenient way to reach the baths and navigate Bath's busy streets, as Robert Southey explained: 'There being in some places no carriage road, and in others so wide a pavement that in wet weather there would be no getting at the carriage, sedan chairs are used instead... [*the*] chairmen... wear large coats of dark blue.' In 1813 the chairmen charge 6d to carry you 500 yards and 1s 6d for 1 mile (1.6 km). You may see invalids using a 'gouty-chair'. This comfortable wheeled chair, designed by John Joseph Merlin, is steered by the invalid using two rotating handles attached to the wheels.

Invalids receive their daily internal dose of Bath water at the Pump Room, which opens early in the morning. It costs a guinea per month to drink the water, plus a tip for the 'pumper' who serves it from the marble vase on the south side of the room. The recommended dose is a maximum pint and a half (852 ml) per day. But you only drink half a pint at a time; invalids take two doses in the morning before breakfast, and the last portion at noon. Benjamin Silliman did not enjoy his small sample of Bath's celebrated water: 'The taste... is slightly chalybeate [*tasting of iron*], and disagreeably warm, exciting the idea of an emetic.'

New arrivals to Bath write their name in the visitors' book kept in the Pump Room. This entitles you to subscribe to the weekly balls and assemblies. In *Northanger Abbey* Catherine Morland is disappointed that handsome Henry Tilney's name 'was not in the Pump-room book... He must be gone from Bath.'

From midday, including Sundays, people crowd together at the Pump Room to meet friends and parade up and down the room while the orchestra plays. Catherine Morland and her friend Isabella 'eagerly joined each other' in the Pump Room in Bath 'as soon as divine service was over'. But after discovering that the crowd there was 'insupportable, and that there was not a genteel face to be seen... they hastened away to the Crescent, to breathe the fresh air of better company.'

After a stroll in the Royal Crescent, North and South Parades, or Sydney Gardens, or a trip to the shops in Bath's own Bond Street, visitors return to the Pump Room. Balls are held twice weekly at the Upper and Lower Assembly Rooms in season; card games are played on the other nights of the week, except Sunday, when the rooms are opened for promenading. The theatres are open in the evening after dinner, or you can listen to a concert in the Upper Rooms (also known as the New Assembly Rooms). In 1812 a ticket for all nine concerts at the Upper Rooms in the winter season costs two guineas.

You'll love exploring Sydney Gardens and its '16 acres of pleasant walks, waterfalls and pavilions, pretty bowers and small delightful groves', according to *The Historic and Local New Bath Guide* (1812). The Kennet and Avon Canal runs through the gardens; two Oriental-style bridges span the cut. A winding labyrinth leads to a 'grotto of antique appearance'; there's also a sham castle, bowling greens and swings. Jane Austen enjoyed a gala night at Sydney Gardens in Bath in June 1799. In a letter to Cassandra she wrote: 'the fireworks... were really beautiful; the illuminations too were very pretty.'

If you are too infirm to travel by coach to a watering-place you can install one of the recently invented 'shower-baths', which can be used as a vapour, steam or water shower. The hot water or steam is supplied by a coal-fired boiler. The *Repertory of Arts, Manufactures and Agriculture* (July 1813) reported that Dr James Cumming's 'vapour, fumigation, or shower-bath, adapted, at a small expense, for the use of public hospitals or private families' costs about a penny a day to run. The patient sits inside an apparatus akin to a large beer or cider barrel with a seat inside; a tap at the bottom of the barrel allows the water to drain away.

THE SEA-CURE

If 'taking the waters' doesn't work, the 'sea-cure' may be more efficacious. In Austen's unfinished novel *Sanditon*, Mr Parker is carried away by the tide of his enthusiasm for its briny benefits:

> The sea air and sea-bathing together were nearly infallible, one or other of them being a match for every disorder of the stomach, the lungs or the blood. They were anti-spasmodic, anti-pulmonary, anti-bilious and anti-rheumatic. Nobody could catch cold by the sea; nobody wanted appetite by the sea; nobody wanted spirits; nobody wanted strength... If the sea breeze failed, the sea-bath was the certain corrective; and when bathing disagreed, the sea breeze alone was evidently designed by nature for the cure.

Fashionable resorts include Brighton, Cromer, Margate, Scarborough and Weymouth. Invalids drink seawater (very nasty) as well as bathing in it. If you feel brave enough, try a hot sea-bath followed by a dip in a cold-plunge bath. Less hardy souls go for a drive or walk afterwards instead. In August 1812 John Dickenson and his wife Mary (née Hamilton) went to Southsea; Mary 'bathed in the hot sea-bath for the first time and took a long airing afterwards.'

Brighton (formerly Brighthelmston) first rose to fame for its sea-bathing in about 1750, when Dr Richard Russell popularised seawater as a cure for scrofula and other health problems. Russell moved his practice to Brighton, and soon lodging houses for invalids appeared in the town. Since the Prince of Wales began frequenting the town in 1782, it has become even more popular with people of fashion.

According to John Feltham's *Guide to All the Watering-places*, (1813) visitors to Brighton can enjoy the 'hot and cold baths... near the Steyne... On one side of a handsome vestibule are six cold baths; and on the other hot baths, sweating, and shower-baths'. Ladies who want to bathe in the sea go to 'the east side of the town, and gentlemen to the west. Thus decency is preserved.'

You may see a 'Fly-By-Night' or 'Man-Fly' (c.1809) on the Brighton streets. This tiny carriage with four wheels is drawn by one man at the front, while another pushes the vehicle from behind. The 'Fly-By-Night' earned its name because the Prince of Wales and his friends often put one to good use during their midnight larks. Most invalids continue to use sedan chairs, however.

Sea-bathing is such fun that you may lose your sense of decorum. Traveller Richard Ayton was shocked when he visited the genteel resort of Parkgate, Cheshire in 1813:

> Few of both sexes thought it necessary to hide themselves under the awning of bathing machines: posts, with ropes fastened to them, are fixed into the sands, and these were taken possession of by numerous groups of women, six or seven in a row, jumping, ducking, laughing and screaming, evidently as careless of being seen as of being drowned.

Resorts such as Sidmouth and Lyme Regis are also popular; Jane Austen visited Lyme Regis in 1803 and again the following year. In a letter to Cassandra (14 September 1804) she wrote: 'The bathing was so delightful this morning and Molly so pressing me to enjoy myself that I believe I staid [*sic*] in rather too long.'

In *Persuasion*, Anne Elliot and her companions explore Lyme and its environs, and their hearts are lifted by its romantic views: 'The walk to the Cobb, skirting round the pleasant little bay, which, in the season, is animated with bathing-machines and company; the Cobb itself, its old wonders and new improvements, with the very beautiful line of cliffs stretching out to the east of the town, are what the stranger's eye will seek.'

The 'happiest spot' for a visitor to watch 'the flow of the tide' is nearby 'Charmouth, with its high grounds and extensive sweeps of country, and still more its sweet retired bay, backed by dark cliffs.' You can sit for hours gazing at 'the woody varieties of the cheerful village of Up Lyme; and, above all, Pinny, with its green chasms between romantic rocks… where a scene so wonderful and so lovely is exhibited… these places must be visited, and visited again to make the worth of Lyme understood.'

And with so many beauties like these to choose from in Jane Austen's England, surely you'll want to return again and again.

APPENDIX 1

Biographical Sketch of Jane Austen

Jane Austen was born at Steventon Rectory, Hampshire, on 16 December 1775. She was the daughter of clergyman George Austen and Cassandra Leigh, who had eight children: James, George, Edward, Henry, Francis (Frank), Cassandra, Jane and Charles. George suffered from fits and does not seem to have lived with his siblings.

The Austens were a respectable middle class family. George Austen was not poor, but he had to support a wife and eight children on limited means, and often borrowed from other family members in order to stay afloat.

Jane was devoted to her sister Cassandra, so they were sent to school together when Jane was about six or seven years old. Their mother commented wryly that if Cassandra was 'going to have her head cut off, Jane would insist on sharing her fate.' The girls were placed with a Mrs Cawley at Oxford; the school later moved to Southampton, but both sisters became ill from a 'putrid fever' and Jane almost died. Despite this setback, the girls were sent to the Abbey School, Reading, run by a Mrs Latournelle.

When Jane was about nine years old, the sisters came home to finish their education; Jane had the run of their father's library. She began writing skits and stories, and her family greatly encouraged her work. Between 1795 and 1798 Jane wrote early versions of three novels: *First Impressions*, *Elinor and Marianne* and *Susan* (later revised and published as *Pride and Prejudice*, *Sense and Sensibility* and *Northanger Abbey*).

Meanwhile, (as we have seen), her older brother Edward was adopted in 1783 by some relatives, the childless Mr and Mrs Thomas

Knight of Godmersham Park and Chawton. Edward became his heir and in 1812 added Knight to his surname.

In November 1800 Jane suffered a huge shock when without warning, her parents announced that the family was moving to Bath for George's retirement. Family legend says that Jane fainted away when told the news. The Austens' stay in Bath was not one of Jane's most creative periods. She began a new novel, *The Watsons*, but it was never completed.

After George Austen's death in 1805, Jane, her mother and sister Cassandra were left with little money. Jane's brothers rallied round with financial help so that the ladies had enough to live on. They left Bath the following year and embarked on a series of visits to family and friends; they lived in Southampton for a time. Then in 1809 Jane's life changed for the better when Edward Austen-Knight offered his mother and sisters Chawton Cottage, a pretty house in Hampshire, as a home.

Once back in her beloved native county, Jane began writing in earnest again. She published four novels during her lifetime: *Sense and Sensibility* (1811), *Pride and Prejudice* (1813), *Mansfield Park* (1814) and *Emma* (1815). Her books were published anonymously, as it was not considered genteel to be an authoress. But her identity soon leaked out, primarily owing to her brother Henry's inability to keep a secret. Jane's novels were well received: *Emma* was favourably reviewed (anonymously) by Sir Walter Scott in the *Quarterly Review*.

Early in 1816 Jane Austen began suffering from a mysterious, recurrent illness, possibly Addison's disease. Despite her intermittent illness, Jane revised her novel *Persuasion*, and early in 1817 she also began work on a new novel, *Sanditon*. In March 1817 Jane told her niece Fanny Knight that she had 'something ready for publication', (i.e. 'ready for the publisher') – *Persuasion*.

By May Austen had become so unwell that her family persuaded her to move from Chawton to Winchester, so she could have the benefit of the best medical care available. Jane and Cassandra took lodgings in College Street, a short walk from Winchester Cathedral.

Mr Lyford, the local surgeon, had a very good reputation. Typically,

Jane tried to make light of her situation. She joked bravely in a letter (27 May 1817) to her nephew James Edward Austen-Leigh: 'Mr Lyford says he will cure me, and if he fails, I shall draw up a memorial and lay it before the Dean and Chapter, and have no doubt of redress from that pious, learned, and disinterested body.' Sadly, although Mr Lyford effected a temporary improvement in her condition, a few days later he admitted that Jane's case was 'desperate'.

Jane Austen died on 18 July 1817. Her brothers Edward, Henry and Frank, and nephew James Edward accompanied Jane to her last resting place at Winchester Cathedral. *Persuasion* and *Northanger Abbey* were published together posthumously later that year.

APPENDIX II

Timeline of Key Events

1764	George Austen marries Cassandra Leigh at Bath
1775	England at war with America
	16 December: Jane Austen born at Steventon, Hampshire
1778	France openly joins American War of Independence
1783	Treaty of Paris – peace with America and France
1793	France declares war on Great Britain
1801	Austen family moves to Bath
1802	Treaty of Amiens – peace with France
1803	Britain declares war on France
1805	21 January: George Austen dies at Bath
	21 October: Battle of Trafalgar and death of Lord Nelson
1806	Jane, Cassandra and Mrs Austen move to Southampton
1809	Austen ladies move to Chawton
1811	6 February: George, Prince of Wales becomes Prince Regent
	October: *Sense and Sensibility* published, written by 'A Lady'
1813	January: *Pride and Prejudice* published
1814	May: *Mansfield Park* published
1815	18 June: Battle of Waterloo and defeat of Napoleon
	December: *Emma* published (1816 on title page)
1817	18 July: Jane Austen dies at Winchester
	December: *Northanger Abbey* and *Persuasion* published together (1818 on title page)
1820	29 January: Death of George III

APPENDIX III

Notes on the Text

Quotations from Contemporary Works
Extracts from Austen's letters are quoted where appropriate from the *Biographical Notice of the Author* by her brother Henry, which accompanied the first edition of *Persuasion* and *Northanger Abbey*; Lord Brabourne's 1884 edition of Jane's letters; the *Memoir* by her nephew James Edward Austen-Leigh (1871); W. and R.A. Austen-Leigh's *Life and Letters* (Smith, Elder & Co., 1913), and J.H. and E.C. Hubback's *Jane Austen's Sailor Brothers* (John Lane, 1906).

Quotes from the letters of Eliza de Feuillide (née Hancock) are from W. and R. A. Austen-Leigh's *Life and Letters*. Quotes from Austen's unfinished novels *The Watsons* and *Sanditon* are taken from Austen-Leigh's *Memoir* (1871).

I have quoted from contemporary works and unpublished archival collections in order to create as accurate a portrayal of Austen's England as possible. However, I have also quoted freely from Austen's novels as well as her letters to help illustrate the times in which she lived. Although one could argue that fiction is only a reflection of real life, Austen's observations of society were exceptionally astute, (though she was not infallible).

The Value of Money in the Regency Period
The question of personal income played an important role in Austen's works: the marriageability of her heroes and heroines depended on it. Because of inflation, it is extremely difficult to give exact modern monetary equivalents for personal incomes and the prices of everyday

necessities in Georgian times. Prices fluctuated greatly between 1775–1820 owing to the Napoleonic wars and unreliable harvests.

I have used the currency converter on the Historical UK Inflation and Price Conversion website to estimate modern-day price equivalents: *http://safalra.com/other/historical-uk-inflation-price-conversion*. This currency converter is based on Jim O'Donoghue, Louise Goulding, and Grahame Allen, 'Consumer Price Inflation Since 1750' (ISSN 0013-0400, Economic Trends No. 604, pp 38-46) 2004).

For example, in *Pride and Prejudice* (1813), Mr Darcy's 'personal estate' of £10,000 p.a. would approximate to an income of £610,000 p.a. at 2013 prices, so he would still be a highly eligible bachelor today.

APPENDIX

Bibliography

Unpublished Sources

Accounts of the Machell family of Hollow Oak in Pennybridge and Haverthwaite, 1775, Lancashire Archives DDMC 28/5

Chester Chronicle (on microfilm), 14 September 1810, Cheshire Archives and Local Studies

Diaries of Dolly Clayton of Lostock Hall (1777, 1783), Lancashire Archives DDX 510/1–2

Diaries of John Egerton of Bunbury (1826) Cheshire Archives and Local Studies DDX 597/2, DDX 597/3

Diary of Daniel Vawdrey junior (1792–1793), Cheshire Archives and Local Studies DMD/N/1/7

Diary of Margaret Pedder (c.1789), Lancashire Archives DDPD/25/16

Journal of a Tour of Hampshire 1812, John Dickenson (2nd), Lancashire Archives DDX 274/9

Journal of Benjamin Wyatt (1790), Cheshire Archives and Local Studies DMD L/2/3

Receipt Book of Mrs Owen (18th-19th centuries), Lancashire Archives DDX 337/1

Contemporary Works

Newspapers, magazines, pamphlets and Parliamentary papers

Accounts and Papers relating to the Increase and Diminution of Salaries in the Public Offices of Great Britain...year ending 1 January 1815, [182], VIII, 1815

Amusing Chronicle, or Weekly Repository

Annual Register for the Year 1809, Vol. 51, London, 1811

Annual Register for the Year 1811, Vol. 53, London, 1825

Annual Medical Review and Register for the Year 1809, Vol. II, London, 1810)

'Ancient and Modern Travelling', *Railway Times for 1839*, London, 1839

Anti-Jacobin Review, and True Churchman's Magazine, June-December 1813, Vol. XLV, London, 1814

Athenaeum, or Spirit of the English Magazines, October 1817 to April 1818, Boston, 1818

A View of London, or the Stranger's Guide to the Metropolis 1803–4, London, 1804

Belfast Monthly Magazine January to June 1812, Vol. 8, Belfast, 1812

British Mercury or Annals of History, etc., Vol. 7, Hamburg, 1788

Daily Journal, or the Gentleman's, Merchant's and Tradesman's Complete Annual Accompt-Book, London, 1790

Edinburgh Annual Register for 1808, Vol. 1, Part 2, J. Ballantyne & Co, 1810

Edinburgh Annual Register for 1811, Vol. 4, Part 2, J. Ballantyne & Co, 1813

Edinburgh Practice of Physic and Surgery (no author), London, 1800

Encyclopaedia Brittanica (no author), 6th edition, Vol. 6, Archibald Constable & Co., 1823

Essay on Quackery, Kingston-upon-Hull, 1805

European Magazine and London Review Jan to June 1792, Vol. 21, Philological Society of London, 1792

The Examiner, No. 314, 2 January 1814

Gentleman's Magazine, Vol. LVI, Part I, London, 1784

Gentleman's Magazine, Vol. LVI, Part II, London, 1784

Gentleman's Magazine, Vol. 62, Part II, London, 1792

Gentleman's Magazine, Vol. LXXVI, Part I, London, 1806

Gentleman's Magazine, Vol. LXXXIII, Part II, London, 1813

Gentleman's Magazine, Vol. XCIII, Part 1, London, 1823

Gentleman's Magazine, Vol. 138, Part II, London, 1825

Gentleman's Magazine, Vol. XXI, New Series, Part I, London, 1844

Gentleman's Magazine January-May 1868, Vol. 224, 1868

Hampshire Chronicle, 13 November 1809

Kentish Gazette, 6 April 1810, 12 November 1811

Kilmarnock Mirror, or Literary Gleaner, Vol. 1, Kilmarnock Press, 1819

La Belle Assemblée, Vol.I, Pt. I, London, 1806

La Belle Assemblée, Vol.I, Pt. II, London, 1806

La Belle Assemblée, Vol. III, London, 1807

La Belle Assemblée, Vol. II, New Series, London, 1810

Lady's Magazine or Entertaining Companion for the Fair Sex, Vol. XII, London, 1781

Lady's Monthly Museum Vol. 1, Verner & Hood, 1798

Letters from an Irish Student in England to His Father in Ireland, (no author), London, 1809

London Magazine, Vol. XLIV, London, 1775

London Magazine Enlarged and Improved Vol.2, London, 1784

Monthly Magazine, or British Register, Part II, Vol. XXIV, London, 1807

Monthly Magazine, or British Register, Part I, Vol. XXXIII, London, 1812

Monthly Magazine, or British Register, Part I, Vol. XLIX, London, 1820

New Annual Register or General Repository of History, Politics and Literature for the Year 1799, London, 1800

New Complete Guide to All Persons Who Have Any Trade or Concern with the City of London (no author), 16th edition, London, 1783

'Notes on Dandies', *Once A Week*, Vol. X, Bradbury & Evans, 1864

Penny Magazine, Charles Knight & Co., 1837

Public Characters of 1803–4, (no author), Richard Phillips, 1804

Repertory of Arts, Manufactures and Agriculture, Vol. XXIII, Second Series, 1813

BIBLIOGRAPHY

Report from the Select Committee on Anatomy, [568], Vol. VII, 1828

Report from the Select Committee on the Supply of Water to the Metropolis, [537], 1821

Repository of Arts, Literature, Fashions etc., Vol. IV, R. Ackermann, 1817

Repository of Arts, Literature, Fashions etc., Vol. V, R. Ackermann, 1818

Spirit of the Public Journals for 1801 Vol. V, (London, 1802)

The Sporting Magazine, Vol. 14, London, 1799

The Sporting Magazine, Vol. 35, London, 1810

The Sporting Magazine, Vol. 3, New Series, London, 1819

The Times, 22 October 1816, 28 October 1816, 2 November 1816

Books

Adams, Samuel and Sarah, *The Complete Servant: Being a Practical Guide to the Peculiar Duties and Business of All Descriptions of Servants*, Knight & Lacey, 1825

(Anon.) *A Biographical Memoir of the Public and Private Life of the ... Princess Charlotte Augusta of Saxe-Coburg*, John Booth, 1817

(Anon.) *A Picture of London for 1802*, R. Phillips, c.1802

(Anon.) *Domestic Economy, and Cookery, for Rich and Poor*, Longman, Rees, Orme, Brown and Green, 1827

(Anon.) *The Trial of Jane Leigh Perrot*, Taunton, 1800

Apperley, Charles J. ('Nimrod'), *The Chace, The Turf and the Road*, 2nd edition, John Murray, 1843

Austen, Jane, *Emma: A Novel*, Richard Bentley, 1833

Austen, Jane, *Northanger Abbey: A Novel*, and *Persuasion*, Richard Bentley, 1833

Austen, Jane, *Mansfield Park*, Richard Bentley, 1833

Austen, Jane, *Pride and Prejudice: A Novel*, Richard Bentley, 1853

Austen, Jane, *Sense and Sensibility: A Novel*, Richard Bentley, 1833

Austen-Leigh, J. E., *A Memoir of Jane Austen... to which is added* Lady Susan, *and Fragments of Two Other Unfinished Tales by Miss Austen*, 2nd edition, Richard Bentley & Son, 1871

Ayton, Richard and Daniell, William, *A Voyage Round Great-Britain Undertaken in the Summer of the Year 1813*, 1819

Badeau, Adam, *Aristocracy in England*, New York, 1886

Barrett, Charlotte (ed.), *Diary and Letters of Madame D'Arblay*, Vol. 2, Philadelphia, 1842

Barrett, Charlotte (ed.), *Diary and Letters of Madame D'Arblay 1793–1812*, Vol. 6, Henry Colburn, London, 1846

Beresford, John, *The Miseries of Human Life*, Vol. II, London, 1807

Berkeley, The Hon Grantley F., *My Life and Recollections*, 4 Vols., Hurst & Blackett, 1866

Blackman, John, *A Memoir of the Life and Writings of Thomas Day*, London, 1862

Blew, William C. A., *Brighton and Its Coaches*, John C. Nimmo, 1894

Brabourne, Lord Edward, *Letters of Jane Austen*, 2 Vols., Richard Bentley & Son, 1884

Bradley, Dr T., (ed.), *Medical and Physical Journal June-December 1803, Vol. X,* London, 1803

Brayley, Edward Wedlake, and Britton, John, *The Beauties of England and Wales, Vol. X, Pt. 3: London and Middlesex*, London, 1815

Burke, Sir Bernard, *A Genealogical and Heraldic Dictionary of the Landed Gentry of Great Britain and Ireland*, 2 Vols., London, 1863

Burney, Fanny, *Camilla, Or A Picture of Youth*, 5 Vols., London, 1802

Burney, Fanny, *Cecilia, Or Memoirs of An Heiress*, 5 Vols., London, 1786

Burney, Fanny, *Evelina, Or A Young Lady's Entrance into the World,* 2 Vols., 1829

Byron, Lord George Gordon, *Works of Lord Byron*, Paris, 1828

Cary, John, *Cary's New Itinerary*, 2nd edition, 1802

Chapman, Maria Weston (ed.), *Harriet Martineau's Autobiography*, Vol. 1, James R. Osgood & Co., 1877

Colchester, Lord Charles, *Diary and Correspondence of Charles Abbot, Lord Colchester*, 3 Vols., John Murray, London, 1861

Colvin, Sidney, (ed.), *Letters of John Keats to His Family and Friends*, Macmillan & Co., London, 1891

Cooke, Rev Thomas, *Universal Letter-Writer* (London, 1812)

Cooley, Arnold J., *The Toilet and Cosmetic Arts in Ancient and Modern Times*, London, 1866

Corry, John, *A Satirical View of London*, 6th edition, London, 1815

Crell, A.F. and Wallace, W.M., (eds.) *The Family Oracle of Health*, 6th edition, J. Walker, 1824

Cromwell, Thomas Kitson, *History and Description of the Parish of Clerkenwell*, 1828

Edgeworth, Maria, *Belinda*, 3rd edition, 3 Vols., London, 1811

Edgeworth, Maria, *Tales and Novels, Vol. XVII containing Harrington, and Thoughts on Bores*, London, 1833

Edgeworth, Maria, and Edgeworth, Richard Lovell, *Memoirs of Richard Lovell Edgeworth Esq.,* Vol. 1, London, 1821

Egan, Pierce (ed.), *Grose's Classical Dictionary of the Vulgar Tongue*, Sherwood, Neely & Jones, 1823

Egan, Pierce, *Sporting Anecdotes*, London, 1820

Elliott, Robert, *Gretna Green Memoirs*, London, 1842

Erredge, John A., *History of Brighthelmston* [sic], Brighton, 1862

Espriella, Don (Southey, Robert), *Letters from England,* 3rd edition, 3 vols., 1814

Faulkner, Thomas, *A Historical and Topographical Description of Chelsea, London*, 1810

Feltham, John, *Guide to All the Watering and Sea-Bathing Places*, London, 1813

Foster, Vere, (ed.), *The Two Duchesses: Georgiana Duchess of Devonshire, Elizabeth Duchess of Devonshire, Family Correspondence...,* Blackie & Son Ltd, 1898

BIBLIOGRAPHY

Gilpin, William, *Observations on Several Parts of Great Britain, particularly the Highlands of Scotland made in the Year 1776*, Vol. II, 3rd edition, (London, 1808)

Gilpin, William, *Observations on the Western Parts of England, Relative Chiefly to Picturesque Beauty* (London, 1808)

Goede, C.A.G., *The Stranger in England*, 3 Vols., London, 1807

Good, J.M., Gregory, O., and Bosworth, N., *Pantologia, Or a New Cabinet Cyclopaedia*, Vol. IX, London, 1819

Graham, Dr J., *Medical transactions at the Temple of health in London in ... 1780*, 1780

Griffith, S.Y., *New Historical Description of Cheltenham*, 2nd edition, Vol.1, Longman, Rees, Orme, Brown and Green, 1826

Gronow, Capt, *Recollections and Anecdotes of the Camp, the Court, and the Age of Clubs*, Smith, Elder & Co., 1864

Hamilton, Edwin B., *Record of the Life and Death of Princess Charlotte*, London, 1817

Harris, James Howard (3rd Earl), (ed.), *Diaries and Correspondence of James Harris, 1st Earl of Malmesbury*, Vol. III, Richard Bentley, 1844

Hazlitt, William, 'The Letter-Bell', *The Mirror of Literature, Amusement and Instruction*, 12 March 1831, Vol. 17, 1831

Heron, Sir Robert, *Notes*, 2nd edition, London, 1851

Holt, Edward, *Public and Domestic Life of... George III*, 2 Vols., Sherwood, Neely & Jones, 1820

Horne, Thomas (tr.), and Goede, C.A.G., *A Foreigner's Opinion of England*, Boston, 1822

Huish, Robert, *Memoirs of George IV*, 2 Vols., London, 1830

Jackson, Lady (ed.), *Diaries and Letters of Sir George Jackson*, K.C.H., 2 Vols., Richard Bentley & Son, 1872

Jackson, Lady (ed.), *The Bath Archives: A Further Selection from the Letters and Diaries of Sir George Jackson, K.C.H*, Richard Bentley & Son, 1873

Jamieson, Alexander, *Universal Science: or the Cabinet of Nature and Art*, 2 vols., London, 1821

Jesse, Edward, *Anecdotes of Dogs*, London, 1858

Jesse, Captain, *The Life of George Brummell*, 2 Vols., Saunders & Otley, 1844

Jervis, John and Kitchiner, Dr William, *The Traveller's Oracle, or Maxims for Locomotion*, 2 vols., London, 1827

Kirby, R.S., *Wonderful and Scientific Museum, or Magazine of Remarkable Characters*, Vol. 1, London, 1803

Kotzebue, Augustus von, *Travels from Berlin, through Switzerland, to Paris, in the Year 1804*, Vol. 3, London, 1804

Lanfear, Mrs, *Letters To Young Ladies On Their Entrance Into the World*, (London, 1824)

L'Estrange, Rev A.G.K., *Life of Mary Russell Mitford*, 2 Vols., New York, 1870

Luttrell, Henry, *Letters to Julia, In Rhyme*, 3rd edition, (John Murray, 1822)

Lysons, Daniel, *Environs of London: County of Middlesex*, Vol. II, 2nd edition, London, 1810

MacPherson, David, *Annals of Commerce, Vol. IV, London*, 1805

M'Donogh, Felix, *The Hermit In London: Or Sketches of English Manners*, 3 Vols., London, 1821

Moore, Thomas, (ed.), *Letters and Journals of Lord Byron*, Frankfurt, 1830

Moritz, Charles P., 'Travels Through Various Parts of England in 1782', William Mavor (ed.) *British Tourists; or Traveller's Pocket Companion*, Vol. IV, London, 1814

Newdigate-Newdegate, Lady, *The Cheverels of Cheverel Manor*, Longmans, Green & Col, 1898

Nicolas, Sir Nicolas Harris, *Dispatches and Letters of Lord Nelson*, Vol. 7, Henry Colburn, 1846

Oulton, W. C., *Travellers' Guide, or English Itinerary*, 2 vols., 1805

Parkes, Mrs William, *Domestic Duties: Or Instructions to Young Married Ladies*, Longman, Hurst, Rees, Orme, Brown and Green, 1825

Parnell, Sir Henry, and Telford, Thomas, *A Treatise on Roads*, Longman, Orme, Brown, Green, and Longmans, 1838

Paterson, Daniel, *Paterson's British Itinerary*, 2nd edition, 2 vols., 1807

Pennant, Thomas, *The Journey from Chester to London*, London, 1811

Perkins, John, *Every Woman Her Own House-Keeper, Or The Ladies' Library*, London, 1796

Phillips, Sir Richard, *A Morning's Walk from London to Kew*, London, 1817

Pückler-Muskau, Prince (attr.) *A Tour in England, Ireland, and France in 1826, 1827, 1828, and 1829*, Philadelphia, 1833

Reece, Richard, *The Medical Guide*, 15th edition, Longman, Rees, Orme, Brown and Green, 1828

Rennie, James, *A New Supplement to the Pharmacopoeias of London, Edinburgh, Dublin and Paris*, 3rd edition, London, 1833

Reynolds, Frederick, *Life and Times of Frederick Reynolds, Written by Himself*, 2 vols., Philadelphia, 1826

Roberton, John, *A Treatise on Medical Police, and on Diet, Regimen, etc.*, Edinburgh, 1809

Romilly, Sir Samuel, *Memoirs of the Life of Sir Samuel Romilly*, 3 vols., John Murray, 1840

Russell, Lord John (ed.), *Memoirs, Journal and Correspondence of Thomas Moore*, 8 Vols., Longman, Brown, Green, and Longmans, 1853

Shelley, Lady (ed.), *Shelley Memorials: From Authentic Sources*, Smith, Elder & Co., 1859

Silliman, Benjamin, *A Journal of Travels in England, Holland and Scotland... in the Years 1805 and 1806*, 2nd edition, 2 vols., Boston, 1812

Simond, Louis, *Journal of a Tour and Residence in Great Britain, During the Years 1810 and 1811*, 2 vols., 2nd edition, Longman, Hurst, Rees, Orme and Brown, 1817

Stanhope, Eugenia (ed.), *Letters written by Philip Dormer Stanhope, Earl of Chesterfield, to His Son Philip Stanhope Esq.*, 4 vols., Dublin, 1775

Strutt, Joseph, *Sports and Pastimes of the People of England*, 2nd edition, London, 1810

Thomson, William, *A Tour in England and Scotland in 1785,* London, 1788

Tilloch, Alexander, *Philosophical Magazine and Journal*, Vol. LIII, London, 1819

Timbs, John, *Curiosities of London*, London, 1855

Trusler, John, *The London Adviser and Guide*, 2nd edition, London, 1790

Walker, John, *A Critical Pronouncing Dictionary and Expositor of the English Language*, New York, 1823

Wallis, John, *London: Being a Complete Guide to the British Capital*, 4th edition, Sherwood, Neely & Jones, 1814

Wilkes, John, *Encyclopedia Londinensis*, Vol. V, London, 1810

Wollstonecraft, Mary, *Thoughts on the Education of Daughters*, J. Johnson, 1787

Wraxall, Nathaniel William, *Memoirs of My Own Time*, 2 Vols., London, 1815

Young, Arthur, *A Six Weeks' Tour Through the Southern Counties of England and Wales*, London, 1769

Modern Works (published after 1900)

Ackermann, R., *Microcosm of London, or London In Miniature*, 3 Vols., Methuen & Co., 1904

Adamson, Donald (ed.), *Rides Round Britain: John Byng, Viscount Torrington*, Folio Society, 1996

Adkins, Roy and Lesley, *Eavesdropping On Jane Austen's England*, Little Brown, 2013

Austen-Leigh, W. & R.A., *Jane Austen: Her Life and Letters*, Smith, Elder & Co., 1913

Aslet, Clive, *The English House*, Bloomsbury Publishing, 2008

Barchas, Janine, *Matters of Fact in Jane Austen*, JHU Press, 2012

Borer, Mary Cathcart, *An Illustrated Guide to London*, Robert Hale Ltd, 1988

Brander, Michael, *The Georgian Gentleman*, Saxon House, 1973

Buck, Anne M. (ed.), *The Gallery of English Costume Picture Book No.2, Women's Costume: The Eighteenth Century*, Art Galleries Committee of the Corporation of Manchester, 1954

Buck, Anne M. (ed.), *The Gallery of English Costume Picture Book No.3, Women's Costume 1800–1835*, Art Galleries Committee of the Corporation of Manchester, 1952

Burnett, John, *A Social History of Housing 1815–1970*, Methuen & Co., 1980

Byrde, Penelope, *A Frivolous Distinction: Fashion and Needlework in the works of Jane Austen*, Bath City Council, 1979

Calder-Marshall, Arthur, *The Grand Century of the Lady*, Gordon & Cremonesi, 1979

Chapman, R.W., *Jane Austen: Facts and Problems*, Oxford University Press, 1970

Chapman, R.W., *Jane Austen's Letters*, 2nd edition, Oxford University Press, 1952

Cole, Hubert, *Beau Brummell*, Granada Publishing, 1977

Collins, Irene, *Jane Austen and the Clergy*, Hambledon & London, 2002

Day, Malcolm, *Voices from the World of Jane Austen*, David & Charles, 2007

Downing, Sarah Jane, *Fashion in the Time of Jane Austen*, Shire Publications, 2013

Edgcumbe, Richard, (ed.), *The Diary of Frances, Lady Shelley* (1787–1817), John Murray, 1912

Ewing, Elizabeth, *Fashion in Underwear*, B. T. Batsford Ltd, 1971

Filbee, Marjorie, *A Woman's Place*, Book Club Associates, 1980

Hadfield, Charles, *British Canals: An Illustrated History*, Phoenix House, 1959

Harman, Claire, *Fanny Burney: A Biography*, Flamingo, 2001

Hartley, Dorothy, *Water in England*, Macdonald & Jane's, 1978

Henson, Louise, *Culture and Science in the Nineteenth Century Media*, Ashgate Publishing, 2004

Home, James A. (ed.), *Letters and Journals of Lady Mary Coke*, Vol. IV, Kingsmead Reprints, 1970

Hubback, J.H. and E.C., *Jane Austen's Sailor Brothers*, John Lane, 1906

Jameson, Peter (ed.), *The Diary of James Woodforde Volume 17 1800–1802*, Parson Woodforde Society, 2007

Kloester, Jennifer, *Georgette Heyer's Regency World*, Arrow Books, 2005

Lane, Maggie, *Jane Austen and Food*, Hambledon Press, 1995

Laver, James, *Fashion and Fashion Plates 1800–1900*, King Penguin, 1943

Le Faye, Deirdre, *A Chronology of Jane Austen and Her Family*, Cambridge University Press, 2006

Le Faye, Deirdre, *Jane Austen: A Family Record*, 2nd edition, Cambridge University Press, 2004

Le Faye, Deirdre (ed.), *Jane Austen's Letters*, 4th edition, Oxford University Press, 2011

Le Faye, Deirdre, *Jane Austen's 'Outlandish Cousin': The Life and Letters of Eliza de Feuillide*, British Library, 2002

McLynn, Frank, *Crime and Punishment in Eighteenth Century England*, Routledge, 2002

Mingay, G. E., *English Landed Society in the Eighteenth Century*, Routledge, 1963

Mitton, G.E. *Jane Austen and Her Times*, Methuen & Co., 1905

Monson, Lord and Leveson-Gower, George, (eds.), *Memoirs of George Elers*, D. Appleton & Co., 1903

Mullan, John, *What Matters in Jane Austen?*, Bloomsbury, 2012

Perkin, Joan, *Victorian Women*, John Murray, 1993

Quennell, Marjorie and C.H.B., *A History of Everyday Things in England, Pt. II, 1500–1799*, 8th edition, B.T. Batsford Ltd, 1948

Quennell, Marjorie and C.H.B., *A History of Everyday Things in England, Pt. III, 1733–1851*, 5th edition, B.T. Batsford Ltd, 1950

Richardson, Albert Edward, *Georgian England*, B.T. Batsford, 1931

Seeley, L.B. (ed.), *Fanny Burney and Her Friends*, Seeley & Co. Ltd, 1908

BIBLIOGRAPHY

Southam, Brian, *Jane Austen and the Navy*, 2nd edition, National Maritime Museum, 2005

Southam, Brian (ed.), *Jane Austen: The Critical Heritage*, Routledge & Kegan Paul Ltd., 1968

Summerson, John, *Georgian London*, Pelican Books, 1962

Taylor, Lou, *Mourning Dress: A Costume and Social History*, Routledge, 2009

Tomalin, Claire, *Jane Austen: A Life*, Viking, 1997

Vickery, Amanda, *Behind Closed Doors: At Home in Georgian England*, Yale University Press, 2009

Vickery, Amanda, *The Gentleman's Daughter: Women's Lives in Georgian England*, Yale University Press, 1998

White, R. J., *Life in Regency England*, B.T. Batsford Ltd, 1963

Wilkes, Sue, *Regency Cheshire*, Robert Hale Ltd, 2009

Wilks, Brian, *Jane Austen*, Hamlyn Publishing Group Ltd, 1978

Williams, E.N., *Life in Georgian England*, B.T. Batsford Ltd, 1962

Winstanley, Roy, 'Skip-Jacks', *Parson Woodforde Society Journal XIX No.1*, Spring 1986

Winstanley, R. L. and Jameson, Peter (ed.), *The Diary of James Woodforde Volume 9 1780–1781*, Parson Woodforde Society, 2000

Winstanley, R. L. and Jameson, Peter (ed.), *The Diary of James Woodforde Volume 10 1782–1784*, Parson Woodforde Society, 2001

Winstanley, R. L. and Jameson, Peter (ed.), *The Diary of James Woodforde Volume 11 1785–1787*, Parson Woodforde Society, 2002

Winstanley, R. L. and Jameson, Peter (ed.), *The Diary of James Woodforde Volume 16 1798–1800,* Parson Woodforde Society, 2006

Woodforde, John, *The Strange Story of False Teeth*, Routledge & Kegan Paul Ltd, 1983

Worsley, Lucy, *If Walls Could Talk: An Intimate History of the Home*, Faber & Faber, 2011

Online Sources

Dow, Gillian and Halsey, Katie, 'Jane Austen's Reading: The Chawton Years', *Persuasions*, Vol.30, No.2 (Spring 2010), *www.jasna.org/persuasions/on-line/vol30no2/dow-halsey.html*

Farrer, William & Brownbill, J. (eds.), 'Townships: Egton with Newland', A History of the County of Lancaster: Volume 8 (1914), pp. 358-360. URL: *www.british-history.ac.uk/report.aspx? compid=53330 Date accessed: 03 December 2013*

Manville, H.E., 'The Bank of England Countermarked Dollars 1797-1804': *www.britnumsoc.org/publications/Digital%20BNJ/pdfs/ 2000_BNJ_70_11.pdf*

Index

INDEX

181

INDEX